The Eleven
Who Were
Saved

Author

Bernardo Gomez Restrepo

A MIS HIJOS:

Carmen Eugenia Gomez

Bernardo Gomez

Alberto Gomez

Marco Antonio Gomez

Table of Contents

Chapter 1 The Family of Faith...1

Chapter 2 Love and Loss...31

Chapter 3 The Bonanza 62

Chapter 4 The Fall of Innocence 71

Chapter 5 The Accident...86

Chapter 6 Broken Dreams.. 102

Chapter 7 The Shadow of Sin................................... 115

Chapter 8 New Lands: Union City............................ 131

Chapter 9 Crossroads in Miami 141

Chapter 10 The Vigil at the Hospital 155

Chapter 11 Double Betrayals.................................... 173

Chapter 12 Legacy 188

Final Chapter 30 Years, my Love 192

Chapter 1
The Family of Faith

Berni, the youngest of the eleven children of Don Marco Aurelio, asked his mother when he was only six years old,

"Mom, why aren't my siblings the same as me?"

"Son," she replied, "When siblings are twins, they look very similar to each other, but if they aren't twins, none of them look alike. They might share some traits like hair, eyes, or body type, but none are identical. For example, their personalities, gallantry, voices, and many other details are different. Do you understand, son?"

"Oh yes," Berni answered.

"Look," his mom told him, "my fingers on my hand are all different from one another and have different names. The same goes for my children and those of any other mother."

"Mom," said Berni. "Is it that God makes children so moms don't mix them up? Because how would it be for you, I imagine, with the eleven of us siblings?"

"Hahahahaha. Yes, son, it would be a disaster, and I'd end up completely crazy."

Berni ran out to water the plants and flowers in the garden, just as he did every morning, following his mother's orders.

This is how the story of Don Marco Aurelio's children begins. All were born in the city of Armenia, known as the Miracle City, in the Department of Caldas, formerly part of Old Antioquia, in the Republic of Colombia, South America. It's called Miracle due to its rapid and remarkable development.

1

This is corroborated by the immediate reconstruction after an earthquake in 1999 destroyed most of it, and by the miracles that occurred in the home of Don Marco Aurelio and Doña Carmen.

Colombia is the happiest country in the world, slightly surpassed in joy by the Dominican Republic, another country located in the Caribbean. This makes the region of America even more beautiful—the bride of the world.

This sense of joy and warmth is something Berni carried with him as he flew to New York. He had always felt a deep connection to the region's festive spirit, especially at Christmastime. However, as American Airlines flight 961 from Miami made its way through the stormy skies over the Northeast, Berni couldn't see the city's famous skyline. The rain was relentless, driven by a storm that had battered the area since early December 23, 1984—exactly Berni's birthday. It was the third time he had come to visit his wife and children, always ensuring that his visit coincided with Christmas so that he could share in the celebration of another anniversary of the birth of Jesus of Nazareth.

The last time, a year earlier, he had seen them in Miami, but now they were living in Union City, New Jersey, just a few miles from New York via the Lincoln Tunnel, which connects the two American states.

Berni got off the plane, headed to baggage claim, and once he had his luggage, he went to the taxi stand. Boarding one, he asked the driver to head to Union City, handing over the address where his wife and children—Carmen, Bernardo, and Alberto—now lived. Berni was dropped off a few steps from the spot, but it was enough to get him soaked and frozen from the cold, with the temperature at 10°C. He rang the bell twice, and finally the door opened. Maria Eugenia, Berni's wife, appeared, and upon seeing him, she was struck mute. Likewise, her husband couldn't utter a word in greeting—she was pregnant.

One year had passed since they last saw each other during the Christmas season of 1983 in Miami, but Maria Eugenia was now seven months pregnant. Berni could only stammer a few words of greeting to his children. At that moment, Berni's wife vanished. He would never see her again until fate brought them face to face in the waiting room of Baptist Hospital in Miami, awaiting the death of Herman, Berni's nephew, Maria Eugenia's lover, and the father of the child she was carrying.

Bernardo Jr., understanding his father's situation, grabbed a bottle of liquor and offered him a shot, which he downed, followed by another. Berni didn't know what was happening, and it was only a short while later that his son began explaining that his mother had been having sexual relations in their own home with Herman, Berni's nephew.

Berni remained silent, asking no clarifications from his son. Instead, he asked him to accompany him in finding a nearby hotel. But Junior begged him not to go—it was still raining, the night was pitch black, and finding a hotel room would be difficult as they were all full for the end-of-year season. Berni agreed and slept in the same room as Junior, though he only pretended to sleep and couldn't close his eyes all night.

The next morning, Berni rose at dawn and called his son Bernardo, asking for a towel to head to the bathroom. Then he told him to watch for the taxi arriving in half an hour. He went to his younger son Alberto's room. He asked him to pack his suitcases, as he was taking him to Miami for a check-up on the open-heart surgery performed eight years earlier at the Shaio Clinic in Bogotá, Colombia. Half an hour later, they were on their way to Newark Airport, where Berni hoped to catch an early flight to Miami to leave—or try to leave—his nightmare behind. Once he had the plane tickets and boarding passes, they went to the cafeteria and served themselves a modest breakfast from the self-service line.

The plane took off at 10 a.m., heading south, and three hours later, they were exiting Miami International Airport. Jaime, Berni's brother, was waiting at the exit to take them to his apartment. Berni had called him earlier from Newark. Berni immediately expressed the need to find a house to rent or buy, and quickly asked for local newspapers. He also asked Jaime to accompany him that afternoon to the children's hospital to register Alberto for consultations. Berni thanked him in advance for the help.

Berni and his son took a bath, and shortly after, they were in a taxi with Jaime heading to the hospital. Once there, they filled out the registration forms and sat down to wait for the assistants' call. Meanwhile, Berni apologized to his son and stepped out to the garden with his brother. There, Berni told Jaime what had happened the previous night in New Jersey. Jaime lamented his brother's situation and offered help. When Berni asked if he had known about it, Jaime said yes. Berni, very upset, reproached him for not telling him. Jaime replied, "A year ago, I sent a letter to Cali informing him that Maria Eugenia was Herman's lover. She was pregnant, and they moved to New Jersey to avoid a scandal that was already known throughout Miami and Colombia. As always, the husband is the last to know when his wife is unfaithful."

They then returned to the waiting room, and seconds later, Alberto was called by a nurse for pre-consultation exams.

An hour later, Berni was called by the doctor who had seen his son. The doctor told him Alberto was fully recovered from the surgery and could lead an everyday life. Incidentally, he added, the hospital was getting too small for Alberto, who was already showing signs of being a well-developed young man. Berni understood what the doctor meant. The doctor also said he wanted the names of the surgeons at the Shaio Clinic in Bogotá to congratulate them on the successful operation. Berni thanked him for the news and said goodbye. This truly filled Berni and his son with joy. "One day is never like another," he told his son as they left the office, heading to the nurses' station to schedule a follow-up in two months. They approached his brother and invited him to leave. The taxi that had brought them was waiting, and Berni instructed the driver to take them to an American diner for "something to eat," as Colombians say.

Upon arriving, Berni invited the driver too, and they all entered after Berni grabbed a magazine from the dispenser at the entrance—a real estate insert for houses and apartments for sale or rent. At the table, after ordering, they circled house addresses near Jaime's with the driver's help. It was the 402 area, better for distinguished people like you, the driver said. Berni, despite the heartache tearing him apart, told the man those words would double his tip. After eating, they headed to Jaime's house, where they were staying temporarily until finding a place.

Berni cherished life, his wife, his children, and all of humanity, yet an overwhelming sadness consumed him—an aching, profound sorrow that he could scarcely bear.

The next day, Berni set out to find a house for himself, his son, and his secretary, who would arrive from Cali, Colombia, in the coming days.

Berni needed to organize his thoughts to execute the plans he'd devised on the flight to Miami. He soon sat in the living room, ready to go but needing his brother and his car for house-hunting. He waited, feeling his head heavy from the second sleepless night. Jaime soon emerged, asking what kind of house he wanted and suggesting they wait for Lilian, the secretary, as women are best at choosing homes.

"Yes, of course," Berni pretended. "And anyway, Lilian and my son will live there since I don't know what'll become of me."

"Why?" Jaime asked.

Berni replied, "I might return to Cartagena for my businesses after settling things here. Plus, I need to confirm my son's health. I'll also bring Carmen Eugenia and Bernardo Jr. to Miami to continue their studies—this is the best U.S. city for Colombians."

Jaime advised Berni to relax, visit family and friends, and wait for the secretary. That night, they explored discotheques—the best for their lights, décor, and furniture, clearly funded by Colombian mafias, making them world-class. Berni never imagined the sound systems and music. The crowd was distinguished, including notorious Colombian cartel leaders from Medellín, the hub for most U.S.-bound drugs via the Bahamas, Puerto Rico, and Panama. Back then, the Cali Cartel lacked the export power it gained after Pablo Escobar's violent death by police.

Days passed, perhaps a week, and Berni enrolled Alberto in the nearest school upon receiving transfer documents from Emerson School in Union City, New Jersey, where Alberto and his siblings had been studying high school.

Surprisingly, Berni received a late-night call on a Thursday, two weeks after arriving in Miami. Lilian, his secretary, was waiting for her luggage from a flight from Los Angeles. She said she'd be at his brother's apartment in under half an hour and begged him to wait, as she had to update him on everything. Berni waited, and minutes later, after introductions, they went to a nearby restaurant. While waiting for food, Lilian recounted her journey. Berni had planned the entire trip from Cali to Miami, but Lilian didn't know it involved an illegal crossing through Mexico. She had no U.S. visa from the Colombian embassy. Still, Berni said she'd pass legally with a visa issued in Mexico. This was a lie to prevent her from panicking and getting detained or deported at the border or in the U.S.

Lilian started: "The trip was extraordinary—I'm thrilled to be in this beautiful country with its landscapes, roads, and people."

Berni interrupted, asking about the border crossing. She said, "In Mexico, we flew to Tijuana. Diomedes took me to a greyhound racing track."

"True?"

"Yes."

Berni replied, noting such races date back 2,500 years to Egypt.

"We left at midnight, arriving at the border booths an hour later. Diomedes showed documents to the agent. They asked him questions; I only knew where we came from. I said from the dog track in Tijuana."

"In Spanish or English?" Berni asked.

"English."

"How did it go?"

"Perfectly, better than Shakespeare."

"Good," Berni said.

"Then we reached San Isidro, per Diomedes—I had no idea where we were. His sister and family waited there. The next day, to Los Angeles, and you know the rest. But how did you get the visa in Mexico after our struggles in Cali and Bogotá?"

"I remember," Berni said, "but I'll tell later—I got no visa."

"Don't leave me hanging—it's incredible!"

Berni explained post-meal: "There was no visa; you crossed illegally."

"How? I can't believe it."

"It's true, my dear secretary. You're undocumented, but only we, Diomedes, and God know."

The next day, Lilian, updated on house-hunting plans, listed addresses. In Jaime's car, Berni, Lilian, and Alberto toured, following Jaime's brother's traffic tips. Within half an hour, in picturesque old Coral Gables, two police cars and two civilian vehicles blocked them with flashing lights. Seven men emerged—four giant uniformed, armed police; four or five plainclothes with weapon vests. A civilian showed an FBI badge. They asked for Berni's license in English, then pressed them against the car (Jaime's, who wasn't there). Seeing Berni's Colombian license, they scoured the car for over an hour, including Jaime's messy electrician tools. They frisked Berni, Lilian, and Alberto, too. Finding nothing, they asked why they were in such an upscale area. Berni showed the address list for house-hunting. Alberto added in perfect English that they were father, son, and secretary. The officers apologized and left.

An hour later, Berni recovered and drove to Jaime's, deciding to pause the search until tomorrow, heading to 95th Avenue via South 40th Street.

Berni told Jaime that afternoon upon his return from construction. Jaime raged, suggesting a lawsuit. Berni agreed it was a human rights violation but doubted an American judge would uphold it against Colombians in an anti-drug operation. "It's a miracle they let us go—with our 'stigma,' they could detain us for background checks. For Colombians, entry here is already enough."

Lilian, Berni, and Alberto discussed furniture layout in their rented house (with a buy option): three bedrooms, 2.5 baths, a family room, living-dining, kitchenette, front garden with royal palm, two parking spots; a large back patio with lemon and orange trees, a clean canal with fish. Neighbors were 20+ meters away. Ideal spot on 96th Avenue, #96-69, near Jaime's—key for Berni's plans, as Jaime knew the city.

Berni had Lilian call a locksmith to change locks, install door/window alarms, and check electricals. He shopped for tropical furniture and house items. Days later, Lilian had it nicely arranged and decorated—her good taste, order, and cleanliness shining, unlike in an office.

None cheered Berni; the heartache prevented full appreciation.

Lilian, thinking Berni worried only about Alberto's doctor visits, promised to handle appointments by phone. More visits confirmed Alberto's good health.

Berni pressed on, ensuring no future surprises. Fortune-tellers' charlatanry, scientists' conjectures, sages' predictions—world ending, earth freezing, sun scorching, waters drying, ending plant/animal/human life—none knowable.

Berni couldn't have imagined his ordeal. Pondering this, the phone rang at 10 p.m. His sister from New Jersey said Maria Eugenia had a cesarean the previous night; the baby was wrapped in the umbilical cord around the neck, dead for a week. Death's shadow hung over the "home" of Berni's wife and nephew, Herman Muneton (the father). The child had a layette, room, and more ready—Herman was financially well-off from businesses (illicit or not) rising for a year.

This spurred Berni to accelerate plans. Two weeks and many calls later, he met his nephew Fernel at the airport from Cali. After greetings, they headed to "the progressing city," where Fernel introduced three drug-world contacts. One agreed on how, when, where, and price.

A week later, Fernel returned to Cali, only to discover— unexpectedly—that his wife was "out of base" (cheating). In a fit of rage, he sent her to University Hospital. Infidelity, it seemed, had become an epidemic.

A month passed; Berni instructed Lilian on his two children's arrival (Carmen Eugenia, Berni Jr.) from New Jersey—pick them up at the airport. Berni couldn't wait; he needed Cartagena by next Saturday for business after two months away. Lilian knew; Berni trusted her. He asked her to pack as he showered to dress for the airport. Then two patrol cars arrived, lights flashing. Two burly cops rang at 9669. Alberto opened; they asked for his father. Berni appeared. They showed badges, asking two questions. "Sure," Berni said.

(They blocked the door.)

"Know Mrs. Maruja?"

"Yes, officer."

"At Baptist Hospital yesterday?"

"Yes."

"Come to the station for more questions."

"Gladly."

Berni told Alberto to tell Lilian to finish packing—they'd wait, he'd be back in three hours max. He said it before the cops, but wasn't

9

sure. He entered the first car's back; another unseen agent sat there. The conversation was cordial in bad Spanish with the agent.

Berni is the youngest of eleven children from Doña Carmen and Don Marcos's legal marriage. Born on December 23, 1939, in Milagros town on the Central Cordillera's slope, south of Antioquia, one of Colombia's largest departments. The land was cool and humid, with coffee as the main product. Beautiful estates housed the world's best coffee crops, with some cattle. The people were Catholic and healthy, but they also believed in old Antioquia myths like "Guacas Boar"—an infernal-spirited pig that protected fields and livestock. Myths like the dwarves, "Single-Legged Witch," and headless friar also influenced local behavior. Myth writers like Javier Ocampo López claim that Colombian mythological topography is among the most significant, extensive, and beautiful in the world. This country, still seen by some Europeans as purely indigenous, is a planetary wonder: its people, cordilleras, three seas (Atlantic, Caribbean, Pacific), natural riches, fauna, flowers, birds, coal, oil, gas, gold, and emeralds. Colombian women are considered the most beautiful and sensual in the universe, akin to those in Venezuela, France, and Italy. Uniquely, saints perform miracles, and whores, unashamed, carry mats under their arms for directness.

Berni was born after one of the worst earthquakes the region had suffered, and only 10 years after the worst economic crisis in the world, caused by the United States.

The Second World War was unfolding among the economic powers when, the night before the anniversary of the Birth in Bethlehem, the home of the most charming and admired marriage was filled with joy at the arrival of a child, baptized eight days later by Father Botero as Berni. (Why give him that name? Let's name him Jesus, Juan, or Pedro, said the priest, but Don Marcos, who was a man of few words and spoke clearly, replied by raising his thunderous voice, "I've named him Berni, Father.")

The next day, a commission from the board of directors of the convent of the Sisters of Charity arrived at Doña Carmen's house and, upon seeing such a beautiful child—docile, quiet, blonde with green eyes—they begged the proud mother to allow them to place him that night in the very crib of the Nativity scene the nuns had created for the Christmas festivities. They wanted to represent, in the most original way, the birth of the Divine Child, as they expressed to Doña Carmen.

"It is an honor you do me," said Doña Carmen. "And a blessing from God," she added.

The child was already three months old, and his personality was beginning to show. His father, Don Marcos, said, "Look at him— he's quiet, smiles when he should, and isn't a crybaby like all the children his age."

"No, Don Marcos," said Don Nicolás, the owner of the neighborhood store—"what happens is that our children are better than other people's children."

"Don't be a fool, man," Don Marcos refuted him and quickly left.

The child filled the sweet home of Don Marcos and Doña Carmen with joy. He wasn't one too many, as there were already ten children. Everyone carried him, one of his little sisters dressed him, another combed him, and the eldest washed his diapers and crib clothes. Doña Carmen and Don Marcos never imagined, nor could a fortune teller predict, how much they would suffer throughout their lives because of their eleven children. All were different, obedient, respectful, but they carried a flaw—the males, which was discovered only after the first seven years of the youngest child, Berni, the one who would uncover such a terrible evil that, many years later, would be known as a genetic disease.

Some of them would go on to cause severe wounds in the heart— those lesions that only a mother's heart can heal. Because the father could never heal them. The parents didn't know how to forgive.

The children of Doña Carmen were born without defects. They were brilliant, measured in speech, but quick in action. In love and conquest, they became well known in their town, and people showered them with all the affection they could offer to their fellow beings.

11

Doña Carmen belonged to the association of San Vicente de Paul. She was a member of the Association of Widows with Dignity. She loved God and was active in the association of devotees of the Heart of Jesus, Patron of Colombia. Don Marcos had the best construction contracts for residences for the most famous rich people in the area; he was awarded the contract for the construction of all the stations, with their respective warehouses for the Pacific Railroad, which extended its lines. Electric and parallel rails ran through the department of Caldas, later called the department of Quindío. He was an honest man, serious, and fulfilled in all his duties as a husband, father, worker, and citizen. Descended from the Antioqueño race, a genuine caste, enterprising, who rose with the Sun to work and created wealth with pick and shovel as tools, forming large and beautiful cities like Medellín, Manizales, and Armenia. But in the history the world knows, only the kidnappings, deaths due to explosions, and executions from the mafia, tragically created by the infamous Pablo Escobar and the extraditables, are remembered. At least his grandparents died, says a poem, without knowing what one of their sons would do to Antioquia and Colombia. Even in hell, he went to cause problems with his eccentricities and installed air conditioning even there.

Doña Carmen had a beautiful young lady of only 16 years old. She had skin the color of African pearls, medium height, a slender and agile body, black wavy hair, honey-colored eyes, long curly eyelashes, a large nose, and a full mouth.

One Sunday, two of her friends arrived to request permission from her mother to attend the gathering that took place in the park of the sector every weekend. For such an event, the neighbors gather, mainly the young people, to meet others and form friendships. It was an excellent opportunity to make oneself known and flirt freely. The women go north to south, and the men in the opposite direction. Suddenly, a handsome man, opposite her, fixed his gaze on her eyes. With his blue eyes and serene look, he left her in ecstasy. She was so impressed that she had to suspend the walk and go home immediately, thus missing the concert where "Symphony No. 5" by Beethoven was to be played. The black girl, as they affectionately called her, could not walk due to the trembling of her legs after seeing

12

that young man, who was ten years older than her. At home, she stayed reclined in bed and had a green tea infusion prepared for her.

During the week, the young man from the park, affectionately called the "little monkey," had been asking at all cardinal points where such a beautiful woman could live.

Finally, on Saturday, after the encounter, he arrived at her house. His heart was beating so fast that he thought they might hear it. The winds of the June season whispered in his ear that he could love this woman for a lifetime. And so it was.

He arrived at the house, trying to calm himself, and knocked on the door. Although it was open—since it was customary at the time for doors to remain open—it was understood that if the visitor was not known, he had to knock and wait to be received. The house employee greeted him with admiration (he was very elegantly dressed) and asked what he wanted. Don Marcos replied by asking, "Is this where a precious girl lives whom I had the fortune to meet on Sunday afternoon in the 'Rafael Uribe' park?" The employee confirmed but added that Miss Carmen was not at home. Don Marcos begged her to accept a bouquet of red roses and a card with a note written in his handwriting that read, "Marcos, your admirer. With all respect."

He left feeling very sad for not having seen those eyes again, which had disturbed his peace. He went to the "Alhambra" cafe on Bolívar Square in search of a friend to distract him from his curiosity and impatience. "That girl has me crazy," he told Pablo, who accompanied him. Indeed, she was a virgin girl, in the broadest sense of the word, like all young women of the time, just entering sixteen, the primordial age of a woman. She had a rare and exotic beauty.

The little monkey had found just the woman of his dreams. He was smitten.

Once introduced to her family, he resolved to marry her and set the wedding date for December 16, the day in Colombia for the delivery of Christmas bonuses. This would be, for Marcos, the best Christmas bonus he had ever received. Everything was prepared according to tradition, and Father Londoño, who had known the contracting parties in advance, accepted the date. The announcements were made during Mass in the cathedral of Armenia, at that time, in the department of Caldas.

About six months after the crush, the marriage ceremony was celebrated with a full house, where the elegance and beauty of the newlyweds stood out. The parents of the bride (Don Marcos was orphaned of parents; they had died when he was only twelve, which of course made the marriage decision easier) were present, along with brothers, aunts, cousins, and other family members.

The party was sober, but nothing was missing. The couple was the most elegant.

After the celebration, the newlyweds went on their honeymoon to a farm located on the outskirts of Montenegro, a town located four hours by train from Armenia. The place was dreamy with its meadows, rivers, and mountains. Fruit trees and extensive plantings of caturro coffee—the first coffee trees planted in the region as an experiment—offered both high-quality coffee and a beautiful spectacle due to the uniformity of the plants.

One week later, they returned to Armenia to be with their family to await Christmas Eve, also called the anniversary of the nativity of Jesus of Bethlehem, as well as the New Year.

The Christmas bonus that Don Marcos, the little monkey, had for his "adored black," as he would continue calling her, was a beautiful house. It had interior corridors, a garden with all kinds of flower plants, and was located only one hundred meters from the park where he had first seen her.

He had built it for her, only for her, because, according to him, each of his children would make their own house.

A year later, Don Marcos was heard saying in the same church where Father Londoño had blessed their marriage,

"Put Julio César on him, Father."

That's what his first child would be called, of the eleven that his beloved wife would give him with love.

They could have avoided them, given them away (those who treated them begged them to give them away), or ignored them, but they were Catholics, apostolic, and Roman.

"I," said Don Marcos, "I am very tough, and I can support them all." It was true. Not only had Don Marcos never lied, but he had been taught to buy baskets of food, as he was the only man in his parents' home. From the age of fifteen, he had worked to support his six sisters. And despite being married, he continued assisting them with all their material needs.

The firstborn would give them the greatest scare of their lives. Four days passed, with both his family and the entire town of Armenia searching for him by land, air, and sea—following the old saying of searching everywhere. Of course, there was no sea, only clean rivers that flowed down, disappearing without a trace.

The situation was that, after 72 hours, rumors began circulating that Julio César must be dead. It was strange that he hadn't appeared or that there was no news of his whereabouts. The only thing in his favor was that he was already 18 years old, which allowed him to leave home. He would later explain this, but on the fifth day, news finally came from a town called Genova—he was there, working as a tailor's assistant, waiting for the family of a pretty girl to give him permission to visit her at home as a boyfriend.

The divine Julio César had left after meeting a young lady he had encountered by chance in a store in Armenia. Not wanting to lose sight of her, he enrolled as one of the passengers on the bus that would take her to Genova. There, he arrived in the same clothes he had been wearing and began working to earn the favor of her family, without notifying his mother and father, who loved him dearly.

The eldest son, the beloved son, without remembering his care as an object and forgetting the keys to a house his father had for him when he turned 21, left his home and everything behind.

Of course, when he turned 21, he returned home, but married and with a precious grandson for Doña Carmen and Don Marcos. They were so, so happy with the son of their son that they forgot to give him the spanking on the buttocks they had promised him in their letters, and much time after his disappearance.

With the years and the schooling he received in his effort to learn a trade that could give him prestige before the parents of his beautiful and female Dalila, Julio César would become one of the best tailors in Genova, Armenia, Cali, and neighboring cities. He designed suits for the most well-known judges and secretaries of justice in Cali, some years later, where he would go to live in search of better economic well-being. Five of his eight children would be born there. For Julio César, absolutely no one—after Jesus Christ, his beloved Dalila, and his children and grandchildren—mattered to him. He made it known many times. Having been one of the worst children of Doña Carmen, he was a good husband and one of the best fathers anyone could ever have. This was not in line with the general rule that "good children are good parents."

On the other hand, his children were among the few who did not cause pain and offense to their parents. Each of them would live exemplary family lives and would come to love their father and mother intensely.

A little more than a year passed, and the second in the rosary of children was born—as it was commonly said—of the marriage of the Gómez family.

"Put *ADALBERTO* on him," said Don Marcos dryly to the priest on duty, who was baptizing that Sunday. It was for a beautiful child who, later at 18 years old, would become the most handsome man in the region. He had green eyes, wavy black hair like his mother's, a thick-built body, pearl-colored skin, and an elegant, strong voice. To complement his appearance, he wore a Gardelian-style hat, which was fashionable among young people at the time, given the fame enjoyed by the Creole singer Carlitos Gardel, the tango singer, whose melodies were popular in the suburbs of countries in the southern part of the American continent and had graced the most elegant salons in the world during the 20th century.

His parents loved him from before he was born. But by the age of 18, he frequented the tolerance zones, where the most beautiful and tender women—those often labeled as "whores"—were found. There, he met the most beautiful of all, a woman named Nieves. From this woman, Adalberto would fall madly in love, and it didn't matter to him that she was a prostitute. His love for her would last a lifetime, much like his brother's love for Dalila and his father's love for his "black one."

He never forgot her. In the last days of his life, just before passing away, he still loved her and sent her money to help sustain her needs in old age. Thanks to some information he managed to obtain, he was able to learn her address, still in Armenia, even after 40 years of having met her.

The children of Doña Carmen grew up, others were born, and some brought grandchildren to life. All in all, they were a happy family. Each one, upon reaching the age of 21 and growing into adulthood (the custom was that minors had to wear shorts—just to the knees—and wait until they came of age, which served as a marker to guide others about who was considered a minor), received from their father, Don Marcos, the key to their house, built by him and his workers, and later, by the entire family. Each one of them had their own space, separate from the others.

Adalberto arrived at the house and, without prior notice, presented his 3-year-old son. The grandparents had never seen him nor even heard of this grandson, who was a clone—the first human being ever to be cloned, at a time when no one, not even scientists, had imagined that an animal could be cloned, let alone a human. Only many years later, perhaps 39 years, did science discover the possibility of cloning in humans, thanks to the study of cells, their nucleus, and their components, such as DNA (Ribonucleic Acid).

"Incredible," said everyone who had the pleasure of meeting him. A primrose child, he was not perfect, only because he was the son of a prostitute.

In fact, he was born from the loving relations of Adalberto and Nieves, two beings who loved each other against all social prejudices, within an eminently Catholic country, a town of honorable people, and a family like that of Doña Carmen's, with many moral values.

But the happiness they felt knowing him and having him was like having had the same child for two occasions, a fortune that other mortals lacked.

The child, also named Adalberto, stayed with them with plans for the future.

However, when Adalberto (the son, not the grandson) married Olga, Nieves demanded custody of the child, after having abandoned prostitution.

The grandchildren, like the children of Doña Carmen, were works of art.

Don Marcos repeated the sentence: "Put *Argemiro* on him, Father." The child did not cry when he received the baptismal water. Don Marcos said, in front of the priest and those accompanying the ceremony, "This is another tough one; he didn't cry either when he came in contact with the water." He referred to none of the three born before, and later, the eight that followed with intervals of 11 months (the difference in time between births, as the quarantine was respected during that time, and a mother could only give birth after that period, a rule called "diet"). Without this period, the children of Doña Carmen would have had only 9 months and one day between each birth.

All were born perfect. They seemed to be crafted with a brush, with love, and nothing was missing nor excessive. Doña Carmen never stopped thanking the Heart of Jesus. He was her guide and her consolation, and in the end, he would calm the headaches they would cause her as time passed. Argemiro would be one of those who would write the most important pages of the history of the Gómez family.

Among the people of the city, Doña Carmen and her children were already very well known.

The "San Vicente de Paul" association had her as an active member, collaborating in the solution of the problems of the "Widows with Dignity" group, created to counteract the effects of the societal problems caused by a "Club of Suicides," which every weekend left two or three ladies widowed. This situation forced the mobilization of other women in their favor, because the majority of them were left in absolute misery. Their husbands, addicted to liquor and gambling, committed suicide after losing all their assets.

For Doña Carmen, this was very easy because she had a strong connection with Jesus Christ through the congregation of devotees of the Heart of Jesus, to whom she spoke without mincing words. When she asked others for help for the widows, no one refused to collaborate, because she said, "With that partner you have, who dares to say no?"

"The needs of others are not subject to postponement, they are not for tomorrow, they are not for later, they are immediate," Doña Carmen always said when someone refused to collaborate.

People couldn't understand how, raising so many children, she still had time to work for others.

All the children of Doña Carmen were very cheerful and kind. Argemiro stood out from the others for his talent and sympathy. Very early, he showed an aptitude for acting and theater. In school, he represented several characters during the boom of William Shakespeare's theater. His friends took him to the street (before turning 21) and at their house, they put long pants on him to pass him off as an adult in places he would have been forbidden to enter. He was, in effect, a **showman**, as they are called in English.

So, he would arrive at the home of a very distinguished family in the city with the surname Ocampo. In this house, his friend introduced him to his girlfriend. She was a beautiful woman, slightly taller than him, with white skin, long black hair, black eyes, long eyelashes, a full mouth with sensual lips, a straight nose, and a sculptural body on two thick, long, perfect legs. She was one of the most beautiful women living within 400 kilometers around.

Colombians often take a friend to the girlfriend's house to introduce her, of course, when she is beautiful. So, when Pedro, the boyfriend of Nohelia, couldn't go, he asked Argemiro for the favor. Time passed, and when Pedro went alone, Nohelia was very sad and complained to her boyfriend about the absence of Argemiro. Shortly after, she asked Pedro not to return, as she had fallen madly in love with Argemiro. At his request, she wore a bun tied back, making her look like a lady of the aristocracy.

She was the daughter of a respectable marriage from Tebaida, a town near Armenia, "The Miracle City" of Colombia.

On the day he turned 21, Argemiro formalized with his girlfriend's parents the wedding date, which would take place in the next three months.

He got married, and like his father, nine months later, he already had his firstborn.

In the tolerance zone, where Adalberto was the king, and in gatherings that focused on great philosophical, religious, and sexual themes, he got drunk, trying to solve others' sentimental problems. But Argemiro could not fix his own when he needed it. Between rounds of drinking, he consumed the anticipated inheritance that his wife Nohelia had received from her parents.

On the other hand, Argemiro also went to live in Buenaventura, a port city, with his wife and their first two children. Doña Carmen raised them, and they left just when they had barely grown their feathers, as she sadly used to say when she became melancholic.

"It doesn't matter, everyone must live their own life, and it's better that they quickly free themselves from their mother's skirts," Don Marcos would say when she complained about being abandoned.

In any case, the house of El General would never be empty. In the corridors ran three charming and angelic girls. The eldest of the daughters was named Lucila, followed by Luzmila and Miryam. Each one was different from the others, both in physical traits and natural character. The first was pale, tall, with chestnut-colored hair, big hazel eyes, and well-defined features. Her body was slender. Luzmila looked more like a German or Swedish nymph than a Colombian, blonde with blue eyes, a round little face, and rosy porcelain skin. Her body was chubby and small, light in her walk and in her thoughts. For that reason, she gave herself, before marriage, to the only love of her long life. She would be the first woman of that era to cause the greatest scandal among the inhabitants of the city, which, by then, was ceasing to be a town of love and peace.

Then came Miryam, "the skinny one," as they nicknamed her, and indeed she was. But she had something very original about her—she did things without being noticed. She had the silence of tombs and more variety than a cemetery. Her black hair, her black eyes, her very white skin, and her agile body, with the voice of a nightingale. And when she spoke, she sang.

Joy and harmony had already become permanent in the house of the Guzmáns. Some moved away, and others arrived—children, grandchildren—the family kept growing.

Suddenly, without anyone ever having imagined it, something very serious happened. Doña Carmen had the custom, since the week after her marriage, of cutting Don Marcos's hair—among many other gestures to show him her love, submission, and care. But one Sunday morning, as she was combing him after finishing the cut, she found a louse egg, called a liendre (a term from Cervantes, instead of the usual "liendro"). Unable to control the fury and the trembling of her whole body, she showed it to the little monkey, almost shoving the egg into his eyes and slapping his face with the other hand. She accused him of having another woman and demanded he tell her her name.

"That lousy woman must have something very intimate with you, sir," she said, raising the tone of her African voice, still clear, and demanded that he confess what kind of relationship he had been maintaining and with whom.

The little monkey didn't understand anything at all; everything was strange vocabulary to him, and he remained silent. He got up from the chair where he had been sitting and went out into the street to avoid responding to the blow she had given him. "Better that way," he would later tell one of his sisters when recounting what had happened with his beloved black woman. Never before had he seen her in such a state of jealous rage.

Doña Carmen, clinging to her daughters, spent the whole week crying until the blindness passed. Upon seeing the image of the Sacred Heart of Jesus, she asked for His counsel. She then went to the church and confessed everything in sacred confession to Father Londoño, the parish priest of the cathedral.

The priest stood up and assigned her penance:

"Go back to your house and look for lice in your own head. When you find them, go to the Monkey's sisters' house and ask them for forgiveness."

The daughters found six lice and more than eight nits on her, and Luzmilita also had lice and nits. It turned out that the elegant and proud Doña Carmen was the one who was lousy with lice, along with her most beautiful little girl. She had been infected at school.

She sent the message through her other two daughters for her beloved Monito to return home, because she was too ashamed to do it herself in front of her sisters-in-law.

Don Marcos returned home, and happiness reigned again in the household. An atmosphere of peace could be felt, and Don Marcos had no reproaches, so as not to spoil the requests for forgiveness from his beloved black woman.

"I really don't know why I acted so hastily and accused you of being unfaithful," she admitted.

The fidelity of Don Marcos was something that could be guaranteed. He worked from sunrise to sunset, and his labor was so hard that, as soon as he arrived home, he would sit in his rocking chair and fall asleep until dinner. Afterward, he would drink a cup and then fall asleep in bed.

So then—did he really have enough romantic relations to father so many children? Nobody ever knew; he had such discretion and modesty that it seemed he impregnated her with his kisses. Doña Carmen was very fertile, and nine months after Don Marcos's return, he told the priest:

"Name him Gustavo, Father."

Preparations were underway for the first communion of Miryam and Gustavo—as always, two per ceremony—when the worst twist of fate occurred.

The great crisis of 1930 broke out in the city. Indeed, due to the devaluation provoked by the United States in its currency, the domino effect toppled all the other economies of the world. And in that small city of just over 80,000 inhabitants, nestled on the slopes of the Central Cordillera that runs from south to north across Colombia, Don Marcos was left bankrupt.

The construction contracts he was carrying out did not contain the special clause for cases of devaluation of the Colombian peso provoked by foreign nations. In response to his honesty and commitment, he had to sell the three houses he owned in the names of his eldest children—of course, with their signatures—in order to complete the contracts.

When one of his foremen respectfully suggested that he not fulfill them, Don Marcos replied:

"I would rather be ruined than trample on my honor."

This decision would become his letter of introduction in the future.

After four years, Don Marcos managed to buy back his houses, with only a slight difference in the prices. Contracts slipped through his fingers, just as manna slipped through the hands of the enslaved people of Israel in the desert.

The city was making progress. The shops were frequented by the ladies, and the gentlemen could once again be seen in clubs and cafés.

At home, prosperity was evident. It seemed as though money was falling from the ceiling (the interior roof of the rooms). It was something like the miracle of Moses bringing water out of the rocks.

Never before had there been so much money as there was now—under the pillows or the mattresses.

So Lucila, the eldest, began to talk about buying a car to take her younger siblings to school. And indeed, a beautiful, brand-new automobile was purchased from the Chrysler company—not because it was the best, but because it was the only one that could be imported at that time.

But Don Marcos's good faith and reputation had been compromised.

When Don Marcos asked his black woman where all that money was coming from, she told him that, thanks to the trust people had in him and his family, they had been given custody of lottery winnings that Don Ernesto Correa, the neighbor across the street, had received.

"Don Ernesto," said Doña Carmen, "does not want his family to know. Besides, he authorized us to spend whatever we need. In a gesture of affection and friendship, he left that money with us for safekeeping."

"Well," said Don Marcos, "but why didn't he discuss the matter with me?"

"Well," replied Doña Carmen, "he thought that since you are so particular, you would not accept it."

Don Marcos simply made a gesture of approval with his head, adding a muted "aja."

Lucila took advantage of the situation to ask Don Marcos to allow her to work for Don Ernesto, right across from the house, because they had bought a magazine printing machine. Don Marcos never approved that his daughters work, but as a sign of gratitude to Don Ernesto, and because it was a job so close to his house, he accepted.

The machine was so ancient that it could have been the same one used in the printing of the *"Rights of Man"* by Don Antonio Nariño, one of the most important precursors of the Colombian Homeland. The brand had already been erased, possibly to avoid identification, but it was one of the best that were manufactured in Germany, back when the industry made real machines. The case is that, between one magazine and another, 100 Colombian peso bills were printed—just as perfect as those made in dollars by Colombians, 20 years later. If Don Ernesto had known this, he would never have died.

This money went from being fake to genuine. Ten percent of the amounts circulated through Don Marcos's house, known as the "Lottery."

The car that Lucilita bought carried in its trunk suitcases full of counterfeit money, which, after dropping the girls at school, would be transshipped to the taxi driven by Adalberto, before he went to live in the Sultana del Valle. Adalberto, in the company of a friend, went during the night hours to Pereira, the famous "Pearl of the Otún," where a Colombian president, César Gaviria, was born—later to become president of the OAS. Pereira, Colombia, in the 80s and 90s, was much like Hialeah, Florida, in the United States.

In this "pearl," due to its strategic location as a point of entry and exit—north toward Medellín and Manizales, west to Cali and Cartago, and east to Bogotá, Ibagué, and Armenia—the most respectable gentlemen of the Creole underworld converged.

There, the sale of the counterfeit bills was carried out.

This influx of money in Don Marcos's house was what Doña Carmen referred to as "The Lottery" that Don Ernesto had won.

Every Saturday, Don Marcos arrived at 9 p.m., after having shared beers with his workers and officers. These times were used to discuss errors, the quality of materials, and family gossip—topics Don Marcos was always distant from. He would leave once his employees started talking about such matters.

But one night, Don Marcos arrived an hour earlier, at 8 p.m., which was not accounted for by Don Ernesto, who was used to loading a taxi with suitcases every Saturday before Don Marcos arrived.

The taxi driver who brought Don Marcos was a friend of the other driver, and when they met, they greeted each other. Don Marcos, pretending to be asleep, overheard their conversation and learned that every Saturday, they picked up some suitcases to take to Pereira. This public car was different from the one driven by his son Adalberto, who became a public car driver only to get closer to the Tolerance zone, where he could meet his beloved Nieves, the most beautiful prostitute on earth.

Don Marcos entered his house, called his wife, Doña Carmen, after getting into bed, and shared what he had overheard. He then asked her to explain in detail why these strange movements occurred, and why, every Saturday at the same time, two suitcases were picked up from Don Ernesto's house, if he knew that his neighbor never traveled or left his house.

Doña Carmen, having been waiting for so long to tell her Little Monkey what had been happening, seized the opportunity.

Thus, the bonanza era of the Gómez family came to an end.

Lucila could no longer continue in that job, because that same night, Don Marcos gathered his whole family and forbade them from going out into the street, except only to go to school or in his company to another place.

That same night, Don Ernesto learned that Don Marcos knew about the counterfeit bills, and in another taxi that arrived at midnight, he left with suitcases and family to a place no one knew about for 20 years. This would only be discovered by chance when Don Ernesto's wife entered the "San Antonio" drugstore in Señora City, Colombia, where they ended up after practically fleeing from Armenia.

Doña Carmen promised Don Marcos to confess to him in front of all their children during Mass the next morning, the first Sunday of Lent.

On the way, Doña Carmen repented, invoking the heart of Jesus. However, she did not confess the business of the fake bills because she feared that, being a serious crime against the state, the priest might report them to the authorities. She knew, as a devotee of the Sacred Heart of Jesus congregation, that priests often say more than what Jesus truly said on the Mount of Olives.

Amid this bonanza, Jaime, Marco Aurelio, and Lilia were also born.

They were perfect children. One of the great virtues of all Doña Carmen's children was how each one adapted to the others' characters. They were never seen in disputes or problems over anything. Never did any one of them go with a complaint to their mother or father. They had a unique way of understanding each other through mutual love.

This was not difficult, because from their first days of life, they saw how their parents loved each other and demonstrated that love in all possible ways.

Additionally, their parents had a brilliant idea from the first child onward: to buy their toys, their objects of use (like tricycles, for example), and their clothes—but so that the next child would inherit them, and so on. Of course, in the case of the girls, their belongings would only be passed down among them. In this way, each one was aware of who the previous owner was, which facilitated making concessions when necessary.

The harmony in the household was something to be envied by neighboring families.

On Sundays, Don Marcos ordered the entire family to prepare for an outing to the countryside, usually to the river or to a ranch on the road that connected Armenia to the town of Calarcá. "We are so many," said Don Marcos, "that it's unnecessary to invite neighbors or friends." However, one of the friends always slipped in.

Peace, happiness, and well-being were present in the Gómez home.

But, like in the story of Little Red Riding Hood, a wolf can appear anywhere.

Recently, a family had moved from an unknown place to occupy the house that the Correas had left, where, some time ago, the famous machine for making counterfeit bills as genuine had existed.

The wolf was drawn in by the hare-like movements of the beautiful, blue-eyed blonde, Luzmila.

After some greetings, compliments, and gallantries from afar—because, to get to Don Marcos's house with boyfriend intentions, very good godparents were needed—the wolf, with a gentleman's face, sent her a note that read:

"Distinguished young lady,

Allow me to invite you to come to my house this afternoon at 3; the door will be open. I will be waiting for you to tell you how much love I have been feeling for you, your grace, since I had the fortune of seeing you. With respect and admiration, Rugo." (The wolf did not sign, only wrote his name.)

Luzmila could not read the note, which was written on fine paper, because her hands, legs, and whole being were trembling. She hid the note in her lap, sure that no one would discover it, and waited, sitting, to recover from the shock. She had been fascinated with the neighbor since the first day she saw him, but had not thought anything serious, as she remembered her father's instructions. Lucila, her sister, had suffered intensely for the love of a man who could never visit her because Don Marcos kept him away from the house under threat.

Then, fear made her prey. On one side, the opportunity to have Rugo close, and why not, kiss him; on the other, the terror that her father would find out about the note. The fear was so intense that she became sick. She went to bed with a slight fever and stayed in rest for the rest of the day. She ate the note.

The next day, a 6-year-old sister of Rugo delivered another note that said:

"I wait for you in the same place today and every day, until forever.

Rugo."

No one knows how and at what time Luzmila ended up at the wolf's house. There, the man was waiting for her. She gently pushed the door, which was open, stuck her head in, and then entered. At that instant, Rugo appeared and took her by the hand. Luzmila felt as if she was melting or about to fall to the floor. The man told his little sister to go to Don Nicolás's store or warehouse to buy some drinks to toast Miss Luzmila. The nearest store was 10 blocks away.

Rugo began by telling her that he could not bear this situation anymore and that he needed to have her close. Luzmila noticed the girl had left the door open. Without thinking, she ran and nearly fell to the ground. She crossed the street and headed straight to her house.

No one else saw what happened because Doña Carmen was attending some friends to develop plans for the San Vicente de Paul association. The last note remained in Rugo's house, and he picked it up when the beautiful blonde dropped it, slammed the door shut, and then, with his fist clenched, hit the wall, his arm sinking into the stucco.

Only four weeks passed, but it was enough for Doña Carmen's red-haired doll of a daughter to lose her fear.

She had been receiving the notes through Rugo's sister, and they had already become friends. She managed to get her parents to let her cross the street to the wolf's den, and they suspected nothing. In turn,

29

Melba visited Luzmila at her house. One day, after Melba had arranged a meeting with Rugo under the guise of being casual, he showed up and, with all possible humility, begged her to accept his apologies for the harassment he had caused. He promised not to trouble her again and added that he already had a girlfriend.

"How, you already have a girlfriend?" Luzmila asked him, letting him notice the sadness in her voice. To which he replied:

"Well, not exactly. The only one I really want to be my girlfriend is you."

At that instant, he approached her, looking fixedly into her eyes, and sought her lips eagerly. She closed her eyes and opened her mouth to feel him. The kiss truly melted her; she felt her body liquefy, a mixture of honey with white spots of purity, love, and innocence.

Only minutes passed—perhaps 15—and when she became the girl of the Gómez family again, she gathered herself and returned to her body, now that of a woman. Looking around as if she didn't recognize the place, she asked for Melba, almost shouting, but no one answered. There was no one else at home but the two of them. She left without saying goodbye and, walking slowly, arrived at her house. By a stroke of luck, Anatulia, the girl who had been in the service of the family for 20 years, was there. She suspected something had happened but, with the respect she had for everyone, she didn't ask Luzmila what had occurred.

Chapter 2
Love and Loss

Luzmila was very cheerful. She always looked out the window, sang to the wind, and greeted every person who passed by—even if she had never seen them before. Of all the children of Doña Carmen, she was the most spontaneous talker. Her smile was sonorous, and she showed a natural interest in people and things. But since the wolf sank his teeth into her, she was no longer herself, which caused her mother to speak to her with great affection and anxiety, trying to understand what was afflicting her, aside from her prolonged period of menstruation.

Finally, one Sunday, before leaving for Mass, she confessed to her mother what she had done, and Doña Carmen immediately told Don Marcos. That day, it would be the only Sunday that none of the members of the most appreciated family in the entire city would arrive at the city cathedral to attend the Holy Mass ceremony, as they always did. What would be the surprise of Father Londoño when, at the end of the celebration, he ordered the altar boy to go immediately to the Gómez house to find out the reasons for their absence.

Don Marcos got up early and went to the police station to report the scoundrel, and he couldn't reach his work area either. They offered him two policemen, and together with his son Adalberto, who arrived at noon from Cali, where he already worked for the secret police (F-2), they went in search of Rugo. Before Don Marcos ordered that no one leave the house, not even the youngest children who attended school.

The house, once known for its open doors and flowery garden, the home of the most beloved family, was never seen open again. It became a ghost house. Only two people came out, completely covered, with hats and dark glasses, so no one could recognize them. It was Don Marcos and his son, who went out every day at sunrise and returned at night in search of Rugo, who had disappeared as if by magic. A considerable amount of time had already passed—what had been hours now felt like days, and days like months.

The police chief recommended changing tactics:

"Go out to look for him at night, and mount guard on the opposite corners of his house."

They did so, and two days later, they saw him coming at 5 in the morning toward his house, carrying a bundle of what was later known to be his dirty clothes. Without resisting, but held at gunpoint with a revolver on each side of his ribs, he was taken to the authorities. In front of the inspector on duty, he signed a marriage commitment document to avoid trial, scandal, a penalty of six to twelve years in prison, and the loss of his civil rights. It went very well for him, because, aside from all the advantages he achieved, **HE SAVED HIS LIFE**, as Adalberto, Don Marcos's son, later told him. Adalberto had already received several recognitions from the Valle government for his services in favor of the community.

The marriage ceremony was held in a church on the outskirts of the city to avoid further scandal. The priest, after a considerable offering for the "Holy Family," managed to understand the difficult case and performed the wedding without the usual Sunday admonitions. Very few family members attended, and none from the groom's side, as they considered the union a forced one. The godparents were *Smith & Wesson*, caliber .38.

Doña Carmen and Don Marcos believed that their 15-year-old daughter's marriage would be the solution to their pain, but it was not.

The shadow of sin grew in Doña Carmen's heart each day. She said that her house had become more terrifying, darker. "The error of that woman," she said, "has brought us to the gates of hell."

Don Marcos also let out his frustrations one night after returning from searching for the wolf:

"If I had known earlier what that daughter of yours—" (he always referred to her as "our" or "my" daughter) "—had in mind, I would have preferred to do with her what they did with Joan of Arc!"

32

"God keep you," Doña Carmen replied.

Other events would follow that would end the happiness in their home.

Berni was already seven years old. Two weeks ago, he had received his First Communion, alongside his sister Lilia, the last to fulfill this church commandment. Doña Carmen always said, "First fulfill God, then those to whom you owe."

The little one, as they called him (he was the youngest of the children), finished his homework for *Policarpa Salavarrieta* school around 4 in the afternoon, then went in search of his friends to play. More than six boys gathered and decided to go to a nearby construction site, where, as Berni explained, there were many obstacles for them to play on. "Yes!" shouted the others, all around eight years old.

There, they placed a handcart—one used for transporting materials— 10 meters away (about 30 feet), and in line, they ran one after the other. The first boy jumped, placing both hands on the cart, and flew through the air, landing on his feet. It was difficult, but that made it even more attractive for them. Berni, in an unfortunate miscalculation, got too close to the one ahead of him, and with the heels of the boy in front, he received a sharp and precise blow to the lower part of his jaw, lifting him into the air before he fell to the ground unconscious. The impact knocked out his teeth, which he had only recently acquired with much pride; they were his permanent teeth.

Additionally, the blow nearly severed his tongue.

The adventure companions picked him up from the floor and placed him in the same cart, running with him back to the house. The little one was bleeding profusely, much like a bull in the arena.

People ran from side to side, not knowing what had happened, some shouting, others crying.

When they arrived at Doña Carmen's house, two cars were already ready.

They chose a taxi out of shame with Mr. Santacoloma, as it was evident that blood stains would ruin the car seats.

They arrived at *San José* Hospital, and, entering through the emergency section, they laid him on a stretcher. Immediately, the doctors on duty transferred him to the operating room. The little one had regained consciousness in the car, but was still unable to speak or move; he had lost so much blood. The visible inflammation would prevent the operation, and they needed the laboratory results to determine his blood type. Meanwhile, people crowded outside the hospital, and Berni's relatives paced anxiously through the emergency section's hallways. Don Marcos joined the family and, hugging Doña Carmen, tried to comfort her—the same comfort he needed but disguised with strength.

The doctor and laboratory technician approached the little one's parents and gravely told them:

"Only a miracle can save your son. The little one has Hemophilia type A (the most severe). The laboratory sample of his blood has not yet coagulated, and it has been more than 18 minutes since it was taken from his vein."

"What is that?" said Berni's parents in unison, before breaking into tears. The doctors, nurses, and other relatives who were waiting also broke into tears. The chaos was overwhelming.

A while later, the doctors explained that hemophilia was a hereditary disease caused by the lack of coagulants. There are three types: A, B, and the blood disorder. "Unfortunately, we can do nothing to save the child. Only God can save him."

Doña Carmen and Don Marcos, embraced by the other children and relatives, drowned in their tears.

Berni was transferred to the intensive care unit, and the doctors authorized only one person to stay by his side. Doña Carmen remained, and the doctors withdrew, offering a meeting the next morning at 7 a.m. The mother didn't leave her son's side and spent the entire night with her gaze fixed on his face. The little one, who had once looked like an angelic child—much like the baby Jesus in the Nativity scene when he was born on that 23rd night—now resembled a little monster. He was completely swollen, his eyes were no longer visible, and his mouth occupied half of his face. But Doña Carmen stayed there, only waiting for the doors of the hospital chapel to open, so she could go pray to the Heart of Jesus, with whom she was "intimate," as she said, to threaten those who did not help the cause of the "Abandoned Widows."

At 6 a.m., the doors opened, and with the sound of the bells, she knew she could reach the feet of the Almighty.

Doña Carmen was praying before the image of the Heart of Jesus, which she always kept in her room. With the devotion of the truest believer, she said:

"My Lord, Father, You who have the power to give life to the dead and health to the sick, I beg You to have mercy on me, saving my son. If my son dies, even if it is Your will, I would not be able to bear such pain and suffering. The Bible says that death is the payment for sin. I offer my life in exchange for that of my son. He has not committed any sin, and if it is for the original sin, we already erased it from his soul with baptism at birth."

Many years later, when her son, already saved by the love of Jesus Christ and the faith of Doña Carmen, had read the Bible, the Koran, and all that is written about God, he explained to his mother, when they discussed the miracle that occurred with Berni. He said:

"Mother, live peacefully, because there is no such punishment from God to sinners, as most people believe. When you come to understand the reality of the life and death of Jesus, son of Mary and the Holy Spirit, as it is written in the New Testament, you will see for yourself that from these writings, it is clear that there is no punishment, tongues of fire, hell, purgatory, or the other future events the Old Testament speaks of. What you must do is separate what would have happened before Jesus Christ and what will really happen after Him."

The doctors at the hospital instructed the family to undergo a full laboratory exam to determine everyone's blood types, coagulation, bleeding, and all related results. The hematologist told the parents and siblings of the young patient the next morning that the tests performed would reveal their lineage, as hemophilia was inherited from royal families. "It is not surprising that you have blue blood from kings and princes." Upon hearing this, Doña Carmen, who was dying of sorrow, adjusted her corset, pulled her dress up around her waist, and combed her hair with her hands.

The results indeed showed that all the men were hemophiliacs of type A, RH A+. They inherited this from their mother's lineage, the inheritance of kings and tsars, once in Russia, where Alexis, Tsar Nicholas II's son, was known as the first fragile child due to his constant hemorrhages, temporarily improved by Rasputin, the "Mad Monk" from Universal Literature.

A nurse brought Doña Carmen out of her trance to tell her that the doctors were waiting to visit her son. In the room were more than five specialists, including traumatologists, hematologists, surgeons, dentists, and anesthesiologists. The head of the team told Doña Carmen that they were sorry they couldn't do anything for the child.

"His hemophilia doesn't allow for any interventions. We can't even touch him. The blood bank doesn't have plasma, and the blood that could be transfused directly becomes anticoagulant. The factor to stop the bleeding has not been discovered. We are going to leave him in intensive care to observe his reactions. But we repeat, only a miracle can save him. We are sorry."

Doña Carmen couldn't even offer her thanks; she was inconsolable. The doctors left, and she knelt beside her son. Like a madwoman, she ran to the street, took a public service car, and headed back to her house. She entered, said nothing to anyone, took a picture of the Sacred Heart of Jesus from the living room wall, and climbed back into the vehicle, returning to the hospital.

When she reached her son's side, she was petrified. He appeared lifeless. Son of Doña Carmen and Don Marcos, the last and most beautiful child born in recent times, lay there as if dead, but he was in a coma. To anyone who wasn't a doctor, he might have seemed deceased. Doña Carmen knelt beside his bed, placed the image of the Lord on his chest, and, with all her calm, prayed once again to the Sacred Heart of Jesus, asking Him to save him and bring him back to life.

"You can, Lord, and don't tell me you can't."

A while later, she whispered to the child, "Son, the Lord is the only one who can save you and bring you back to life. If you can still hear me, ask Him to grant you the gift of life. I love you, and I can't bear for you to leave."

She fell asleep as she was, for she hadn't slept the night before.

An hour later, the nurse on shift helped her sit up and placed her in the visitor's chair, but she stayed awake, continuing to cry.

The child, in a weak movement, touched the image of the Sacred Heart with his finger, though neither the nurse nor Doña Carmen noticed. He began to speak without words:

"Little God, I know I am going to die, but I don't know how to die. My mom wants me to pray to You, and I don't know how to pray. My mom taught me the Our Father, but I forgot it because I was playing. I remember something, yes, let me see: Our Father who art in Heaven, sacrificed for all of us. I wish that my toys would go to my little brothers, but if I don't die... uff, what a problem, I'll have nothing to play with."

As the child thought this, his heartbeat began to slow again, and his breathing became shallower. The monitoring devices showed that his life was slipping away through the cords that connected him to the unknown, beyond existence.

Doña Carmen was rigid, clinging to her chair, thinking that she had already surrendered to fate, believing that God was punishing her for having taken her son Argemiro when he was about to be ordained as a priest in the Jesuit convent in the holy city of Popayán, in the department of Cauca, in the Midwest of the country.

This had happened only two years earlier. The greatest scandal ever to happen in the beautiful, colonial, and peaceful Popayán, right at the seat of the most sacred place, the Jesuit priest's convent of Colombia.

Indeed, Doña Carmen and her entourage had been the protagonists of the most shameful event ever recorded. This place, after Jerusalem, is the only one where it is easier to find Jesus. Here, it seems He can be seen everywhere, and when one has deep faith, it appears He can be seen both spiritually and physically. The oldest convents and seminaries are here, built in the 14th, 15th, and 16th centuries, before monuments and cathedrals.

It was never known who whispered into Don Marcos' ear that his son Argemiro would be transferred to the convent of the Maricas brothers, and this filled him with rage. According to him, his sons were very masculine, and he preferred to take him out of the convent rather than have him turned into one of those "fancy" gentlemen. With his wife and accompanied by 10 people from the city of Milagro, including a priest, a juvenile judge, and a wealthy businessman, they left one spring morning on an autoferro (a small train) from the Western Railways, which changed vehicles in the Sultana del Valle, to reach the future capital of Cauca by late afternoon, formerly the state of Chibcha.

At the convent, nothing could be done diplomatically to achieve the return of their son. He had been searched for in every corner of the establishment, but he didn't appear. In collusion with the directors and students, and in open defiance, the young man did not present himself before the rector's office, his parents, or the entourage. As the young man was a minor, the parents had full authority, power, and control over such an intelligent, admired, respected, and advanced student. The respectable foundation of the Caiater world had set its eyes on this young man and had plans to make him not only a priest but also a distinguished professor of dogmatic philosophy, religion, and social sciences. In other words, he would

38

be like turning a rough diamond into a polished one, prepared to be the best pope, and perhaps the best because, undoubtedly, he would perform miracles, as he was born in the miracle city of Armenia. Physical miracles, unlike those of previous popes and saints like John XXIII and John Paul II.

After the topic and search were exhausted, the visitors left but returned the next day with an assault team from the army and police, assigned by the authorities of the Holy City after hearing the parents' report of the young man's kidnapping. This led to a warrant for a search and the preventive detention of the rector of the cloister.

This scandalous operation was a shameful act, an offense to clerical authorities, but above all, a grave offense to God. All of this was due to a rumor from a woman in love with the young prodigy who, out of fear of losing him—though it happened anyway—spread false accusations among the people, damaging an entire religious and civil community and depriving Colombian society of having its first **COLOMBIAN POPE**.

The young man was found lifeless but alive due to the cramping of his muscles after having been trapped for over 24 hours in a small one-square-meter space between the ceiling and the roof, a place called the attic located on the balcony of the second floor of the convent.

Indeed, with the tears that drowned her anguish, Doña Carmen remembered. Her conscience began to wreak havoc in her mind, and the gravity of her son's condition took its toll on her. Doña Carmen's head fell upon her chest due to her condition after three days without sleep. Then, several doctors rushed into the room. After a thorough examination, they found that all his vital organs were functioning normally. His pulse, his breathing, and even when they checked his pulse, the doctor found it warm. Opening his mouth slightly, he didn't find the blood clot that intermittently formed inside. The doctor stood up and, looking at his colleagues who were surrounding the sick child's bed, said, "Here, a miracle or something similar must have happened because this child was in a coma and now he is fully recovered." Looking at Doña Carmen, he added, "Your son has been saved."

"Blessed be God!" cried Doña Carmen, and she rushed to her son, kissing him repeatedly, leaving his face wet with tears. Then, she hugged the doctor, kissed him on the forehead, and ran to the hospital chapel where she had been many times before. Fifteen days later, Berni, Doña Carmen's son, was playing with his friends, and supported by both hands, he was holding a pair of wooden stilts more than 5 meters tall, the kind children use to run after others in a competition. This was despite the clear instructions from the doctors and his parents. He was supposed to live a sedentary life to avoid accidents, which could have severe consequences due to his severe hemophilia. One day, Doña Carmen said to him, "Son, you must live as if you were a priest."

"That will never be, dear mother," he replied, and ran off. He lived his life normally, participating in all the risky games. He was free and happy, and his friends called him "The Resurrected." His mother never saw him climb a tree and jump into the river from its branches. He would have fallen there.

The day was beautiful. The sun was shining on the streets, but it was cool due to the spring weather. People went out early, inspired and happy, to fulfill their obligations and duties. Colombia is a country of noble and hardworking people, especially in Armenia, a healthy and Catholic city. But on this day, one that would never be repeated, April 9, 1948, the greatest tragedy since the Holocaust occurred. A historical event that would forever change the history and future of Colombia, a peaceful city like Armenia, and, specifically, it would turn the life of a family upside down. The Gómez family.

Historians call this day the "*BOGOTAZO.*"

It was two in the afternoon when the illustrious Dr. Jorge Eliecer Gaitán fell victim to the bullets fired by the hand of a miserable man. He was in the middle of his political campaign as the sole candidate of the Liberal Party (the "modern" one). It was, indeed, the best and most concrete way to gain power after more than 40 years of Conservative Party hegemony, led by Dr. Mariano Ospina Pérez.

The crime occurred between 1 and 2 p.m., and just an hour later, all of Colombia was in flames. People took to the streets, armed to the teeth, in search of the perpetrators. While the authorities tried to control the crowds, they were killing conservatives one by one. It was revenge by the Liberals against the Conservatives. The latter were not afraid of political power, but of economic power.

It was chaos and total anarchy throughout Colombia. The toll, still undetermined, would leave more than two hundred thousand dead.

Don Marcos was very brave, but he cared more about his family. After the second death threat, and taking advantage of the darkness of the night, he left with his beloved black woman and their children, heading to an unknown destination, even to himself, to avoid telling anyone where they were going to live.

Don Marcos was a genuine conservative, but he was never a fanatic, nor did he abuse or trample on anyone's rights, especially not those of the Liberals. He only demanded from his daughters that they could never have relationships with Liberals, let alone marry them. Before fleeing, he had been locked in his house with his entire family. But food ran out, and the younger children began showing symptoms of dehydration. He and his wife decided they had to flee to avoid death. On the journey, the devoted mother provided her children with a homemade rehydration solution made with water, salt, sugar, and cinnamon, which she carried in her backpack. This, in the end, saved their lives.

In another vehicle, while she saved one of her children, another died. Gustavo, called Paco because of his resemblance to the famous Spanish bullfighter Paco Camino, was irreversibly bleeding in the auto-ferreo speeding toward Cali, the capital of the Valley. The truck carrying the family's furniture and belongings was blocked by a landslide that had fallen the same night they fled, on the road from Armenia to Pereira, called the "Pearl of the Otún." Five kilometers before this beautiful city, more than 50 vehicles were waiting to pass. After the day's work to remove the debris, Doña Carmen's son slept on top of the truck's body, and another man—unaware of the sleeping child—threw the tools and shovel into the air, stepping over Gustavo. Unfortunately, the metal edge scraped his nose, causing a cut of only five millimeters in length but enough to cause a massive hemorrhage. Blood poured out of him like a bull after the second sword thrust in a fight. Gustavo, like all of Doña Carmen's children, was hemophiliac.

Don Marcos's family, not having anticipated this, ended up living in Cali, forced by circumstances.

Hospital San José de Cali—coincidentally, the same name as the hospital in Armenia where Doña Carmen saw her beloved Berni die and then resurrect, thanks to the Sacred Heart of Jesus.

Gustavo was dying too, and again, the doctors couldn't do anything to save him. It was a death...

Doña Carmen went in search of the Sacred Heart of Jesus but did not find it in the churches she visited, including the hospital chapel. No one could tell her where to find it, and it seemed that, in this city, they didn't know God either.

The doctors did not have the coagulation factor to save his life. The plasma had not been separated from the blood through medical science.

The patient vomited the blood that fell into his stomach because he could not even swallow food.

The smell coming from his body was so intense that people could not stay by his side for more than two minutes. His eyes were wide open, and he seemed to ask with his gaze, "Why are you letting me die?" Many years later, the factor 8, which would save the lives of hemophilia patients without the need for a miracle, would be discovered. But there remained the risk of hepatitis or the deadly disease later known as AIDS.

Miracles occur anywhere and at any time where there are people of faith.

Doña Carmen prayed fervently, and when she could not find the Sacred Heart of Jesus, she turned to the Virgin of Carmen, and with her help, she set about trying to save her son. Suddenly, a nurse appeared who was already familiar with the case and had been assisting Gustavo at the hospital. He came to the house and sat down.

"I know a doctor, Dr. Cohen, who is a leading figure in medical science, and he is the only one who can save Gustavo. But the problem is, he cannot enter the hospital; he was expelled simply for belonging to a different religion."

"Do you know where to find this doctor?" asked Don Marcos.

The nurse nodded affirmatively and handed him a card with the doctor's address. The following Sunday morning, the hospital halls and rooms were deserted. A nurse was alone on her isolated shift, sleeping with her eyes open, while the clock showed four in the morning. At the main door, one car followed another, and several men got out. Four armed state security officers went ahead with firm and fast steps, followed by Dr. Cohen, Don Marcos, and his son Adalberto, who was a qualified agent of the Ministry. Behind them followed four more members of the Assault Squad.

They reached the dying patient's room, and immediately the doctor washed Gustavo's face with water and soap, extracted the coagulated blood from his nostrils with a syringe, and then inserted two small soft plastic tubes to clear his breathing. He applied a common plastic bandage to the small wound. The doctor then changed Gustavo's pajamas and bed linens. After washing his hands, he extended one in farewell. He told Don Marcos, "In three days, you'll be home with your family. Eat everything, Gustavo," he added as he was leaving.

The intervention lasted only 20 minutes.

They left the hospital the same way they entered and sped down Carrera Cuarta heading west to drop the doctor off at his house. When Adalberto accompanied Dr. Cohen to the door, he asked how much he owed for the operation. The doctor replied without delay, "You owe me nothing, boy. Go in peace."

Exactly one week later, Gustavo was fully recovering in his room at home, and his mother, Doña Carmen, told him how his salvation had been possible. As she always did, she said with great pride, "God can appear in any form, at any time, and anywhere."

The Sultana del Valle was a region very different from the cool slopes of the central mountain range. The temperature was above 36 degrees, and the people were very expressive, popular, and, to say the least, vulgar, with very liberal customs. It was a city of over a million inhabitants, something like a cosmopolitan urban area, where rapid development was creating some overpopulated areas without infrastructure such as public services, schools, and access roads. These were marginalized places where people of low character could be seen.

Doña Carmen and her children had left behind their relatives and friends in the Miracle City, as well as the associations to which she and Don Marcos belonged. Don Marcos also left behind his workers, his projects, and his clients. But the worst of all was that Lucila, the couple's eldest daughter, had left behind her one and only, greatest love of all time. She had left behind Ernesto, without any clear reason or any clue as to where she had gone to live. She didn't know, nor did her family. This was not the Ernesto whom she worked with (using the printing press to make counterfeit magazines filled with fake bills) but another Ernesto, a humble and hardworking man who had always lived just 100 meters from her house, but 100 light years away from her existence, because he was forbidden from even sending flowers or news, simply because he belonged to a family of Liberals. They had known each other since adolescence, around 13 years old, and had been madly in love, but without the madness of love. Once Don Marcos found out that his daughter's prince was not blue but red, he forbade all contact and also took away Lucila's ability to go out alone. Nothing and no one could change Don Marcos's attitude, despite the godparents who were discreetly sent to try to intervene. This couple suffered intensely, and the young man managed to go to the party's directory and, as a minor, resigned from his party in front of adult witnesses. However, when Don Marcos found out, he did not accept it, arguing that political ideology could not be changed for the love of a woman.

After this, Lucila remained mute for many years, and each day she seemed more like a fabric robot than a human being. Every moment, she died of love for Ernesto. Once in the Sultana, she lost all contact with her beloved, her impossible love, and over time, she succumbed to the fate that offered her no opportunity to see him again. She declared an unannounced hunger strike, no longer laughed, and never accepted invitations to go out with her family. She dedicated herself to working on a sewing machine, speaking to him in the noise, so her father wouldn't realize she still loved him. Whenever someone recommended she rest, she would reply that she wanted to die sewing because it was what she loved the most. Many men approached her with the consent of her parents, but it was like trying to bring life to a marble statue.

The messenger of God, the one who one day brought the news that a doctor he knew could save Gustavo's life, was an old nurse from the San Juan de Dios hospital. He was the only one who, with the patience of old Job, waited for years to get Lucila, the dead woman, to look at him even sideways. The man had fallen so deeply in love with her that he told his coworkers and friends that although she was already dead with love for another, he knew how to embalm her because he had studied the technique of embalming the dead.

Indeed, over time, and after repeatedly visiting her parents' house, where they always expressed deep gratitude for having been the means to save the hemophiliac, she finally looked him in the eyes and became the only man to make her laugh one night when he jokingly said in front of her that he was capable of burying himself alive with a dead woman.

The patient nurse asked her parents for her hand in marriage, trying to ensure her, as she had no idea that he was her suitor or had any such intentions. With the persistence of someone not yet fortunate, little by little, and with great tact, he managed to make contact. Once accepted as her fiancé, he immediately set a wedding date. The poor man spent all his life savings on the trousseau, dresses, and other wedding expenses, including all the formalities. She was more virginal than Mary herself. Even though the parents of the charming, disillusioned girl began to cover the expenses, the sacrifice of the sacrificial man went as far as demanding that the payments be made at his own expense. "This is how we act when we love," he said very clearly.

The best daughter of many good daughters, she wasn't as happy as she wanted to be, but her husband was. Not only because of her loyalty but because, despite not loving him, she gave him five children and would have given him more if she hadn't died young in a dispute with a colleague at work.

The city of Cali had nothing to offer the new residents or political asylum seekers to make them happy. Not only did they arrive directly at the hospital where they were vigilantly waiting for the death of the injured son from the accident near the Pearl of Otún, but they were also forced to wait over 6 hours for their car to pass over the railroad tracks. When they arrived, the passenger train bound for the Holy City of Popayán had just run over a bus with an overcrowded number of passengers, which, after the collision, caught fire. Doña Carmen's children and herself even saw how a passenger from the crashed bus walked without limbs and without a head. Twenty-five people were completely burned to death in the incident.

Don Marcos, as he always did, built the house where his beloved black woman and his children could rest their heads, but from the very first day, they began to lose them.

The car they arrived in, purchased with money from the lottery of counterfeit bills, was sold to raise funds for the exorbitant expenses they were incurring. The buyer was a well-known and wealthy man from the city, but he didn't pay. It became necessary to sue him after all formal collection efforts had been exhausted. The judge overseeing the case ordered the seizure of some of the debtor's property to ensure the payment of the debt. Don Marcos asked his neighbors why there were so many scoundrels in the city, and the people replied that he should not do business with those kinds of people.

Don Marcos managed to recover the money, and miraculously, the lawyer handed him a check a few days after the ruling. He went to the bank and cashed it. The cashier handed him the bills in a bag, and as he was about to leave, the man in front of him in line approached and asked if he was satisfied with the service. Don Marcos replied that he was. At that moment, a pregnant woman, showing signs of fatigue, approached them and asked where she could find the office of the Valley Lottery, as she had made several attempts but couldn't find it. Don Marcos replied that he was new in town and didn't know. The other man present said he knew where it was located. The woman drew them in and, speaking quietly, told them she had won the grand prize of the lottery. Immediately, the other man recommended that she rest a bit because the office was far from there and invited her to come inside the café next to the bank. "Join us," he said to Don Marcos, "because you inspire trust and security," she said in a sweet voice. They went inside and sat at a table. Each of them ordered coffee, but the woman ordered hers with milk and toast. She showed them—almost under the table—the winning ticket and the list of drawn numbers. The men looked closely at the documents, and indeed, the number on the list matched the number on the ticket as the grand prize. To ensure there was no suspicion, there were no alterations in the numbers or the dates. Both Don Marcos and Don José, who had introduced himself earlier, congratulated her warmly, and to celebrate, they ordered two cold beers from the young woman who served them. She said, "Since you seem to be honest people, I'll trust you to collect my prize because I don't feel strong enough to walk to the lottery office. The agency is 10 blocks away." They were both proud of the trust she had placed in them, especially Don Marcos, who was the most respected man in the city. Nevertheless, Don Marcos and Don José insisted that Dona Rosa accompany them, but she apologized for not feeling well and ordered an aspirin.

Don José handed her a package of money, showing its contents, and Don Marcos handed her the bag with the bills from the check, which had not been retained by the lawyer and which he had saved from the lawsuit. She was reluctant to accept it, but they insisted, saying, "We'll return with your lottery money."

The respectable and honest gentlemen left for the agency, not without first paying the café bill.

The woman said loudly so everyone could hear, "I'll be sitting here waiting for you, and may God accompany you."

At the lottery agency, before entering, Don José asked Don Marcos how they could give the money to that woman without knowing for sure whether it was truly a lottery prize or something fake. He added, "You collect it, I'm going with her, and I'll wait for you there. God willing, it's all true. There are scammers everywhere in this city, and it's no surprise if she is one of them."

"If it's true," said Don Marcos emphatically, as if waking from a long sleep, "go ahead, and after being attended to, head straight to the café."

The day passed, and as nightfall approached, Don Marcos, fatigued from going back and forth, returning to the lottery agency, asking about Don José, going to the café, and not receiving any answers to the events that were unfolding, decided to return home.

His wife, very worried, greeted him with a kiss and an embrace and anxiously asked what had happened. Her little monkey, as she called him, replied, "Well, at least I'm okay, and they didn't do anything to me except steal the change from the check."

At the lottery agency, they told Don Marcos that this trick happened regularly and that there was nothing they could do except report it to the police. It was a scam originating from Chile, a country south of Colombia. They told Don Marcos that the winning list was real, and the lottery ticket number was also real, but when looking closely at the document, one could see that the date of the winner was earlier than the ticket's date. "That is," said the agency manager, "they take the list of winners, make new tickets with the prize numbers, and then show them to the victim of the scam."

"Unbelievable," said Doña Carmen. "Of course, the numbers match, and that's why they made you believe they were lottery winners. Brilliant, such clever people."

When Don Marcos and Doña Carmen's children found out about the lottery trick, called the "Chilean Package," they told their parents that with this trick, even Nobel Prize winner Pablo Neruda could fall for this scam. "Don't worry, Dad. God has more to give us than the Chileans can take from us."

48

The phone rang at Don Marcos's house. It was a call from Isla del Cascajal, and on the other end of the line, with a cheerful voice, spoke Doña Carmen's son, who, with an assault squad, had taken Gustavo's savior to the hospital. "Dad, Dr. Luis Granada Mejía is the new Administrator of the Customs Office, and when he recognized your children, he asked for you. Knowing you were without work in Cali, he begged me to bring you so he could appoint you as the head of the delicate merchandise warehouse from abroad, warehouse #4 to be precise. 'The Monkey' is the most honest and capable person I've ever met."

Don Marcos, filled with happiness and pride, ordered his wife to pack their bags to head to Isla del Cascajal, the first port of Colombia on the Pacific. Doña Carmen filled the bags with tears and clothes and went with her entire family and her beloved "little monkey" to Buenaventura, Isla del Cascajal. Immediately, Don Marcos made himself available to the new Customs Administrator. After assuming his position, he went to build the new house where his family would live for more than 20 years, until he retired and moved to a beautiful village located on the slopes of the Western Cordillera, called Lomitas.

Finally, peace and happiness returned to their home.

The nightmare of their unplanned stay in Sultana del Valle, later inexplicably named The Branch of Heaven, was left behind. The house was left to Lucila, the daughter who was handed over to a man she never loved, simply to repay the favor of saving her son Gustavo. However, the one she had truly loved, and would never forget, was Ernesto, the liberal. What Don Marcos never knew was that César, Lucila's husband, was also a Liberal, but he always claimed to be a Conservative because he feared Don Marcos.

Everyone was working, and the younger ones—Gustavo, Jaime, Aurelio, and Jer—were too. Argeqt, who had been living on the Island for over 5 years, held an important position in a transport company, and Gustavo, the survivor, worked for another company. Jaime and Marco worked at the company that managed the port. Dr. worked for a Customs Agency, and everyone contributed money for the well-being of the entire family.

49

Happiness was fully embraced because they were aware that it wouldn't last forever.

Leo Fong was a Chinese man who owned a prosperous motorcycle business on the island. When he met Miss Lilian, the daughter of a local family, she had five strong and sturdy brothers, all in the area, besides those who lived in the Sultana, and a strict, commanding father. He never dared to show up. However, he called each of the brothers one by one and offered them motorcycles. The only condition was that they deliver a greeting to his distinguished little sister, as he would often say. And, indeed, it was better that he didn't show up, for the reputation of the Chinese was that they were Communists, and for a conservative like Don Marcos, seeing a Communist was akin to seeing the devil. "God help him," said Doña Carmen whenever someone commented on the Chinese man.

Having a teenage daughter, beautiful and intelligent, in a port city like Buenaventura, known as Isla del Cascajal, wasn't easy. Don Marcos's daughter was visited by all sorts of men—Liberals, Communists, Conservatives, Socialists, Europeans, Asians, Americans, Muslims—every kind of man. This isn't an exaggeration, because, just like in New York's port, Buenaventura was a crossroads for all races. Ports that were obligatory stops for ships coming from anywhere in the world, with their passengers, crews, and the diseases or vices they brought. Now, it was a suitor who had all the physical characteristics of a blue-blooded prince. He met all the requirements for the most demanding parents of a marriageable daughter.

In this city, there were hundreds of girls who would surely accept this new suitor without a second thought. None other than a prestigious lawyer, a graduate of the University of Santiago de Cali, already renowned for his successes in the civil courts. This man was visiting Don Marcos's family's home.

When Dr. Alomia stood before Don Marcos and, looking him in the eye, declared that he was in love with his daughter Lilia and wished to continue visiting their home as her suitor, Don Marcos, without preamble—true to his straightforward manner—said:

"My dear Doctor, our family cannot mix. We are of pure race, with no mestizos in the family. Therefore, you are free to find a bride elsewhere."

The fabulous prince, wrapped in money but not blue, rather black, never returned to Don Carmen and Don Marcos's home. Jaime, who served as the messenger for his sisters and brothers, carrying messages back and forth, visited the lawyer one day and asked why he never came back to the house. The lawyer replied that Don Marcos had dismissed him because he was black. "That man is an unfortunate racist."

Jaime didn't know what to say and bid the lawyer farewell, never to return to his office.

It was a stormy and rainy Sunday in May, a day without sunshine.

At noon, Arge arrived and gathered the whole family, except for the youngest. He brought the most devastating news the family had ever received. He began by saying they had received a call from the Sultana del Valle, informing them that Gustavo and his wife's brother had been hospitalized after suffering an accident. As soon as Doña Carmen heard the name of the Sultana, she began to pale.

Arge added that they should maintain direct communication with the hospital to arrange travel, but he was hiding the truth. They were already classified with their respective number in the morgue.

Doña Carmen was so affected that, like a robot, she started wandering around the house, going out into the street as if searching for something. People asked her what was happening, and she replied that something was telling her her son had died in that damned motorcycle accident. It was her sixth sense. This helped to move everything along in the house, and preparations were made for the arrival of the bodies. The wake would be for both of them. The other young man was the brother of Arge's wife.

It was later known that the accident had occurred at kilometer 30, which leads from the Sultana to the Island, more precisely on the bridge "La Bruja." The motorcycle was found on the pavement by the driver of a tractor-trailer who, after parking on the side of the road, walked around the site and saw the bodies of the deceased floating in the waters of the small stony waterfall, deep in the background.

These young men were very well-liked in the city, and both were 25 years old. Wherever they went—to a party, café, or bar—they caused a stir, gathering people around them with their great charm. Their disappearance caused much sorrow, and everyone accompanied them to the cemetery.

The trucks, trailers, cars, and buses formed a line of over two thousand vehicles. Both worked for separate cargo transport companies and were well-known to all the drivers who arrived at the port seeking freight.

This is the worst tragedy that can happen within a family—the accidental death of a child. Doña Carmen had 10 more children, but it felt as though she had lost them all. Her pain was immense. She would spend five years crying and two years without holding any conversations with anyone. She only answered what was absolutely necessary. She gave the sad impression that she would never recover from the grief. After much time, and with special treatment through therapy, psychology, and love, she managed to return to the harsh reality, but she would never again be the same Doña Carmen. Dying is natural; dying in an accident is possible, but none of this consoled her. She believed the real cause of her son's death was herself. That was what she held onto. Only a month earlier, Gustavo had been thrown out of the house by his father. Don Marcos expelled him because one drunken night, Gustavo came home around 3 a.m., went to his younger brother Berni's bed, gently lifted the blanket, reached in, and grabbed his penis. When Berni felt this, he raised his feet and kicked hard, unknowingly hitting Gustavo in the darkness of the room. With the noise, Don Marcos came running and took Berni to his mother's bed. There, they heard Berni explain what had happened. Don Marcos grabbed Gustavo by the feet, took him outside, and dropped his clothes on top of him. Gustavo pretended to be more drunk than he was and stayed still. Doña Carmen, knowing Don Marcos so well, didn't argue and allowed him to make his own decisions. In that same moment, Don Marcos told Doña

Carmen that that "sissy" would never enter their house again—at least not while he was alive.

This event made Doña Carmen feel responsible for Gustavo's death. She had done nothing to defend her son. Once, she thought of telling her husband that "Gustavito was probably trying to teach Berni how to masturbate," but she never did.

Doña Carmen's faith began to fade like a lantern running out of oil. She had a grave conflict between what she called punishment and forgiveness. In her mind, the Old and New Testaments collided, and she couldn't accept justice without mercy. Despite all her love for the Sacred Heart of Jesus, she began to think that He wasn't fulfilling His promises. "Could the Lord be sending me these tribulations?" she wondered. She was about to lose her mind when suddenly, a light came into her understanding. She went to the vanity, fixed herself up, which she hadn't done in over two years, put on a dress, and almost ran to the cathedral to find Bishop Gerardo Valencia Cano, one of the most responsible servants of the Lord Jesus Christ. He received her immediately and, in confession, cleared up all her doubts. "The things that happen," he said with clear and advanced understanding, "are not divine designs. They are the results of carelessness, negligence, human error, or mechanical failure. God's project is divine—it was, it is, and will forever be the salvation of the soul through faith."

Doña Carmen felt possessed by the Holy Spirit, as holy as the respected vicar, and, kneeling, asked for his blessing. She then went home, and from that moment on, she returned to being the kind and respected mother of her beloved "little black woman" and wife of Don Marcos.

A few days later, and as promised to the bishop, Doña Carmen returned to him, but this time with her youngest son, Berni. Monsignor asked the boy for his full name, his age, and with only three more questions, placed him on the list of future seminarians for the Archdiocese of Isla del Cascajal and its neighboring towns.

This brought great joy to the devoted mother, and from then on, she saw everything more clearly; she felt a great relief in her conscience

53

because she would return one of her children to God, at least the last one, to make up for the fault she had committed with the Lord when she had taken her son Arge from His hands, just as he was about to be ordained as a priest, only because of the gossip that they were turning him into a "sissy" at the convent.

But as happiness is short, and even shorter for mothers, when Berni learned that the list was meant to send him to the seminary, and knowing his brother's story, which he had not known until that day, he began to chase women to create the reputation of being a sexual pervert, but never a "sissy." He began to regularly visit his brothers' homes and the homes of family friends, seeking his first conquests. He was only 15 years old.

The girl's parents, but worst of all, was her father, Don Marcos, who in cases like this, was the worst of judges; he did not apply justice, but punishment; he didn't listen to reasons, only conclusions; he had a connection to the accused, making him unable to judge the matter. He beat his son so severely that it left him in bed for a month. He forgot that his son was a minor, hemophiliac, respectful, but above all, he forgot that he was his son, and he punished him like no one should punish a dog.

A few days before Berni left for exile, fleeing from his father, his family, and the disgrace of the people, he met Maria, who, knowing everything that had happened, asked for his forgiveness and offered all kinds of excuses. Berni guessed what no one else could: the girl was in love. She promised to accompany him on his trip on the train that would take him to the Sultana del Valle the following day.

On the road that leads from the sea to the Sultana del Valle, there are six tunnels, but one of them is several kilometers long. Berni waited for the opportunity to hide under the table in the train's restaurant car, which he had been sharing with Maria, the former employee of his brother. She covered him with the skirt of her dress, but in the midst of the discomfort Berni was going through, one of his feet stuck out, blocking the passage of the passengers. Just as the car emerged into daylight after the tunnel, and as if planned by the devil, the Bishop of the Island stumbled over Berni's foot. He stepped out to demand an explanation of who had tripped him, only to find himself face to face with Monsignor. After several minutes of silence, the bishop said, "Are you Berni, the son of Doña Carmen?" Berni didn't answer, not because of bad manners, but because he didn't want to explain what everyone had seen. Monsignor asked him to sit with him at the next table, and Berni replied, telling him to wait while he went to the bathroom.

Berni never returned, and the Red Bishop, as the politicians called him, would never see Berni again, who was no longer as angelic as he had been just days before when he was described in front of his mother.

Doña Carmen lost her son Berni. She continued crying and told her beloved "Monito" that she had the impression that she would never see her son again. "I believe," she said, "that the punishment was excessive, and I still have doubts about whether he was responsible for those things, since the girl said he didn't do anything to her!" The "Monito" remained silent but also did not regret his actions. On the contrary, he said, "That's in the past, and what you should do is forget it."

Berni sought asylum from his older sister Lucy, sharing the home with her, her two children, and her husband—the nurse at the hospital where Gustavo, the deceased, had died.

At the Gdez house on the Island, everyone was very sad. Once again, the doors were closed. Invitations for trips to the beach or river came and went, but no one had the desire to go on an outing. Berni and Gustavo left a sad void in their souls.

The most handsome and sought-after bachelors on the Island prowled around the house, seeking an opportunity to win over the now 18-year-old girl, who, as it was believed, needed only the first suitor to begin her journey.

But among all, the one who won the sympathy of the family was a man who appeared suddenly and came from the Sultana del Valle. He was no fool; before even looking at the young and beautiful Lilia, he embraced Don Marcos, greeted Doña Carmen with ceremony, and without even glancing at the future bride, unloaded plantains, yams, potatoes, tomatoes, and oranges that he brought from his farm for the family he called the most beloved on the planet. So he said, and only after that, did he dedicate a minute to Lilia to greet her. Additionally, he unloaded a guitar. When he learned—no one knows how—that there was a very serious suitor of high rank waiting to enter the house to visit Lilia, he agreed with Don Marcos to visit his house every week, and so he did for a long time until, certain of Lilia's love, he set a date for the wedding.

With his guitar and a bit of a voice (for the road dust affected it, as he would tell everyone), he conquered Doña Carmen. She had been lulled by the serenades that Don Marcos used to bring to her house after their marriage, for their love had been at first sight. Again, she remembered all those beautiful moments of her little town. They felt very good with this unknown young man—handsome, polite, and also a musician, although that wasn't his profession; they were sure of this in the bride's house.

After they married, this lovely couple no longer brought vegetables or similar things, and as an excuse, the husband said it wasn't prudent because the guitar could be damaged or broken. After making some inquiries in the Sultana del Valle, they found out that the farm wasn't his, but his father's, and it was no more than a small pasture without cows or horses; there was nothing left there. After this information, Doña Carmen's children named the farm "La Pelada."

This was the last wedding they celebrated in their house. Not the most elegant, though it was, perhaps the wedding of Miryam could have been the best dressed, well-organized, and fulfilled all the requirements. Also, the parents helped with a large portion of the expenses that at that time were typically borne by the bride's parents. Miryam, like Lucila, was another one who sacrificed herself. Like Lucila, she married a man whom Don Marcos and Doña Carmen liked more than Miryam herself, because she was in love with a man named Jaime, whom she loved her whole life. Another one of those suitors who never touched the bride anywhere except for one place, but not on the lips.

In these matters of sex and knowing women, no one, not even any of Doña Carmen's daughters' brothers, can claim to be an expert. But

Lucila was married to the man she loved and would never forget him. Even as the years passed, she recalled him as if time had not passed. She dreamed of him, and sometimes he appeared to her. She would ask what he wanted, expecting him to answer that it was her, but he came from beyond to ask for forgiveness for all the harm he caused her in life. People believed what she said because her Hugo was the worst husband that ever existed. Her male children, born within the marriage, who grew to be four, could not be bad husbands—they were awful. They were exactly like their father in everything, even in their disrespect toward women.

This case, which was widely discussed in society, led to the first studies of genetics. There is much relation between the father and the son, concluded the experts. The extraordinary physical resemblance between the father and his sons was noted. Luzmila spent half her life trying to change her husband without success. Then, she sought help from some relatives to travel to the United States of America. After some time in that country, she managed to bring all five of her children from her own husband to her side. Her only daughter is worth all four men together and perhaps many women in the world. She is one of those true copies of sacrifice, having had her mother by her side since the day she fell ill with severe kidney disease. She receives dialysis treatment every 48 hours at her neighborhood hospital.

Lucila was another of Doña Carmen's daughters, also sacrificed in a marriage of gratitude. She had been taking care of Berni in exile in Cali due to the pneumonia that affected him. But Lucila received bad news from her husband and had to move with her family to Quibdó, Chocó, a department on the Pacific coast, in western Colombia. César, the award-winning nurse, was appointed head of the intensive care unit of the police in Chocó. As a result, Berni had to pack his bags and seek refuge at his brother César's house, the anatomical tailor. His brother's children, his nephews, were contemporaries, and they told him he would have a great time there. Upon arriving in the neighborhood, all the young, beautiful women stirred. Berni was just 18 years old, and the pneumonia hadn't weakened his sexual strength. Weighing 70 kilos and 1.70 meters tall, dressed in oversized clothes from his brother, he was a complete model. The nieces even put their eye on him, though no one knows with what intention.

Once, one of them climbed a four-meter wall without any ladder or help. Once up, she peeked very slowly to observe Berni as he took a shower. Berni noticed her and remained silent, but he understood. She was able to admire him fully. When she was satisfied, she descended as quietly as she ascended. After Berni finished his shower, he went in search of his niece. When he didn't find her, he asked her mother, who replied that the girl was looking for water in the kitchen because she said she was dying of thirst.

Happiness is not everlasting, and once again, Berni was assaulted by the events that had already happened on the Island at his brother Arge's house, where he was accused of attempting something that no one knew what, involving his niece, which caused him illness, the loss of his studies, and, above all, exile.

In these reflections, he decided that the most sensible thing was to leave his brother's house. He went in search of a friend, and with the excuse that his brother's house was too far from work, he convinced him to let him stay in his home, with prior permission from his mother, a dignified widow about 45 years old, with a 15-year-old daughter and a 10-year-old son.

Berni's friend was around 30 years old. He was welcomed with great honor into a distinguished family he had known since the city of Milagro. Berni and Hubert were invited to every party or gathering because they made a great pair, creating a striking contrast. Berni, with his blond hair and green eyes, and Hubert, a strong mulatto with fine features, black hair, and brown eyes, exuded charm and good taste.

Time passed, and Berni went to the medical office for a circumcision after an examination. He had been pressured by his friends, as by his age, he was expected to be free of foreskin. This procedure was said to benefit both him and his relationships in terms of health and hygiene. However, Berni was a hemophiliac, which had delayed the surgery. His mother never allowed it due to the associated risks.

Nevertheless, the day arrived, and Berni lay down for the circumcision. He bled excessively, like a bull in a bullfight. When the doctor finally controlled the bleeding, Berni went home and rested for several days. He took care of himself and changed his own underwear. But one unfortunate night, Hubert's mother noticed bloodstains. She had noticed Berni's strange movements earlier, and now, with this clear sign, she and the others decided to ask him to leave the house. "He must be sick; it could be gonorrhea," they thought, without speaking directly to Berni.

Despite being very delicate due to blood loss, Berni had to get out of bed to pack his belongings. Hubert didn't give a specific reason, but Berni understood, and it wasn't a surprise. His sister, Miryam, listened to his side of the story and welcomed him into her home without question.

At 24, Berni was still the boy of Dona Carmen. He improved his health, and with his nephew, the eldest son of Julio, he began working at a company where he operated a printing press machine. This machine was similar to one in Milagro that had once printed counterfeit bills as genuine. At his new job, they printed cardboard for packaging some of the most famous chewing gums from the United States. The workplace had over 50 beautiful women between 17 and 27 years old. And where there are women, there are problems.

Some of the women started pressuring Berni's nephew to arrange a date with his uncle, as they were all highly attracted to him. With so many options, Cesar didn't know who to give a chance to, but after hearing about it, Berni solved the issue in a Solomon-like way. That same afternoon, after cleaning the machine, Berni took a shower and, without any modesty, walked completely naked among all the women to pick up a soap that had fallen outside the bathroom. They were all amazed and satisfied by Berni's boldness. Even some of the men were impressed. But, as always, jealousy reared its head. The company manager soon called Berni in to pick up his severance check and recommendation letter.

It was on the seventh floor of a skyscraper in the city of Cali where Berni found himself. There, in one of the offices, sat the newly appointed manager of a prestigious customs company. Berni, the son of Dona Carmen, had been offered the management position at this important customs agency. One morning, his brother, the anatomical tailor and father of the climbing niece, visited him and said, "Brother, you have extraordinary luck. After that public display you made, you could've ended up in jail, but now here you are, in this manager's office."

Berni simply responded that times were changing. At just 20 years old, he was the youngest executive in Colombia—and possibly all of America. With his natural intelligence, Berni devised a new way of preparing billing for services to clients. In a novel approach, he charged clients for each bag that was torn at the port or during transport. He also included office expenses, as well as those from the main office located on Isla del Cascajal, even the salaries of employees, proportionally by the ton imported by each client. In this way, he left his employers with the commissions authorized by the local government, clean. The gross profits were automatically the net profits.

His businessman employer provided Berni with a private plane to travel to the island each month to prepare the accounts. During these trips, Berni would also visit his family, who lived on the island at the time. The matter with his niece, Arge's daughter, had already been clarified with his brother, and both had apologized for the misunderstandings. By then, Berni was well-regarded in the city.

Berni was frequently recognized for his managerial abilities, but women continued to cause him to lose his kingdom and wisdom. One day, the building management sent a letter to the owners of the company, informing them that women of all ages paraded daily through the office—none of them were clients—and requesting an investigation. Don Gena, the businessman, became aware of the situation and decided to verify it.

One afternoon, after spending four hours on the island, Don Gena returned early. He opened the office door quietly with his key, peered into the offices, and continued into the next room. There, about three meters away, under the conference table, he found Berni, completely naked with a young woman, no older than 17, whose skirt was over her face. Berni noticed someone had seen him, but Don Gena quickly withdrew, closed the door quietly, took the elevator to the first floor, exited, and rushed to Café Bemoca. There, he called Berni.

Moments later, Berni had dressed and politely asked his visitor to leave, asking her to return another day. After a brief phone call, he joined Don Gena at the café. "From today, start looking for another job," Don Gena said firmly. Berni offered his most respectful apologies. The honorable man accepted them without asking for any explanations. Berni made sure to keep the identity of his visitor a secret, who, without exaggeration, was one of the most beautiful women who had ever visited him under a table.

When it came to orders, there was no need to repeat them to Berni. He quickly began searching for a new job. With many friendships within company management, he invited the manager of an insurance company to lunch. During their conversation, he politely expressed his desire to work for a prestigious company like his guest's. Essentially, he was thinking about marriage and needed to be in an organization where more opportunities were available. His friend was familiar with Berni's capabilities because the customs agency where he worked was also the insurer's representative on the island. On several occasions, Berni had been the subject of discussions between his guest and his superior. Dona Gena and Don Lonso had often commented on Berni's achievements and adventures.

Chapter 3
The Bonanza

Two weeks after the interview, Don Lonso invited Berni to the company and offered him a managerial position, specifically as the head of the car insurance department. In this role, he was responsible for producing new contracts, handling loss adjustments from incidents, managing bonds, and ensuring client satisfaction. Berni was the perfect fit for this position, and the insurer was the best in Colombia's insurance market at the time.

With a salary that doubled what he had earned at the customs agency, Berni moved into a guesthouse. The owner, a respectable lady from Old Caldas, had strict rules—especially against allowing visitors, particularly women, to stay with the guests. This rule was set not only because she had two teenage daughters but also because there were more than 25 single men living there, and she needed to maintain control of her business.

Berni initially hesitated but later realized that a break from his usual sexual activity might benefit his focus on his new job. He accepted. However, it wasn't even two weeks before he introduced the first of his girlfriends to the landlady, explaining that she was one of his sisters who came to collect the money he gave her each month for her studies. The lady asked how many sisters he had, and Berni replied, "Four." He then used this opportunity to ask if he could have his sisters visit him when they came to collect the money, as he helped all four of them. This clever move allowed him to bring four girlfriends into the guesthouse.

Thus began the parade of fashionable women at Dona Rita's guesthouse in Salamina, a respectable lady from Manizales, Caldas, Colombia. Occasionally, nieces—many nieces—would visit, and when they came of age, he introduced them as aunts. On one occasion, the landlady commented on Berni's large family. "Yes, ma'am," Berni responded, "and they call me the Altruist."

A young man working in a business located at the entrance of the building, where the guesthouse was, became friends with Berni. One day, he asked if there was an art studio or modeling agency on the upper floors. Berni smiled and replied that he didn't know but that it seemed like there might be something of the sort.

The landlady would often tell the other guests that Berni was a very charitable man. "He helps all his family, and in front of me, he gives money to each one, telling them not to hesitate to contact him whenever they need help. What a good man he is."

At the insurance company, Berni quickly gained fame—not only for his intelligence and leadership skills but also for his remarkable achievements. During one of his investigations into the loss settlements for goods insurance on imported merchandise, he discovered that the company had fallen victim to a multi-million-dollar scam. This became the subject of a conversation between Berni and the company manager. The manager confidentially asked Berni to keep it a secret but to investigate thoroughly, as the company did not want a public scandal. Berni assured him he was certain about the fraud.

The scam involved a client presenting documents with inflated prices to claim higher indemnities. Berni repeatedly requested the invoices, and the client mistakenly sent them twice. One invoice showed the actual price paid to the exporter, while the other, which they submitted for the indemnity claim, showed double the price. In other words, if a car part cost $5, the invoice presented to claim the loss would show $10.

The insurance company reached an agreement with the importers, who reimbursed the insurer for the excess money paid for the damages. Berni's foresight helped secure the insurer's interests, and in the process, he managed to get permission to sell insurance policies. However, he had to obtain an insurance license from Sena University. To achieve this, he enrolled in the insurance school and attended every day after work. After 10 months of dedication, he graduated with the title "Perfect in Insurance."

Berni's friends, with whom he lived at the guesthouse, began talking among themselves about his special attraction to women, but they couldn't understand why none of his girlfriends seemed to get pregnant. Curious, they placed a bet on who could figure it out. Berni, jokingly, told the curious friend that he had a secret formula that made his sperm die immediately, ensuring no fertilization. The friend didn't quite understand but pretended to, and soon told the others.

Not long after, one of Berni's girlfriends called him, excitedly announcing that she was pregnant. Around the same time, Berni's parents were moving from a small village near the Western mountain range, called Lomitas, to the city of Señora. There, they bought a house and opened a pharmacy business for their beloved daughter, Lucila, who had recently become a widow by the grace of God and her husband. He had been a famous nurse who, as if accompanied by the Holy Spirit, once came to decide who could save Gustavo's life.

This situation would later serve as an excuse for Berni to deceive his girlfriend—the mother of his future child—into waiting for him to finish his family matters before proceeding further.

The nurse, who had left behind five children ranging from 13 years to three months old, had fought for the right to work with his partner at the company. Tragically, during an accident on the job, the nurse fell and hit his head. He was diagnosed with a skull fracture and died 10 days later. This occurred on the island, where they had returned to work after leaving the difficult lands of Chocó, where they had never been happy, especially Lucila, the noble one.

Lucila dedicated herself to her business after obtaining a nursing degree and being licensed by the government. Dona Carmen once again felt immense pride in helping a dignified widow—an especially dignified widow: her own daughter.

Berni, however, was avoiding his responsibilities. One day, his parents, who were already aware of the situation—specifically the pregnancy of one of his girlfriends—asked him to marry her. They left him to decide, saying, "You are of legal age and, as such, are responsible for your actions. We hope your decision aligns with your conscience and self-respect."

Only three days had passed since this conversation when the beautiful future mother of Berni's first child appeared at the door, though she did not enter. She was only three months pregnant and accompanied by her mother and aunt. The young woman had a perfect body, honey-colored large eyes, a well-defined, small mouth, an aquiline nose, wavy black hair, and white skin. She was respectful and fragile, the type of sensual woman who remained grounded. The family commented on how and why...

Maria spoke softly, "I apologize for not notifying you of our visit earlier, but I wanted your son Berni to be present. In the dignity and respect you deserve as women, we hope you understand what we are about to inform you and that you will support my request." Dona Carmen invited them to continue and, without showing surprise, led them to the living room where they sat down. After the usual greetings and an offer of coffee, the topic was broached.

Maria spoke again. "The story of love and dreams is over for me, but not by my will, but by your son Berni, who, after learning of my pregnancy, avoids me with all kinds of excuses! I want to marry him, and I need your help." Dona Carmen, in front of Don Marco, offered her full support. She cried with Maria, admired her beauty, but said that her son was free to choose whether to marry or not, as she no longer had authority over him. Don Marco spoke almost the same words.

They shared a bitter experience with their daughter Luzmila. "A long time ago," Dona Carmen said, "we forced the father of a child our daughter was carrying to marry her. He turned out to be the worst husband in the world, and our daughter became the most miserable of all women."

Dona Carmen recalled those bitter days when her daughter was abused by "that unscrupulous man." It had been a terrifying and sad experience. "Thank God times have changed, and now you come to ask for our help," she continued. "I don't understand why men always avoid this responsibility, even when they are in love. I know,

65

if this is any consolation, that my son loves you, but I think his rejection is because he's too young and wants to remain single, given his success with women. Or perhaps he doesn't feel ready to take on such a great responsibility as a husband and father."

"Exactly," Maria answered, supported by her mother. The aunt, always less reasonable due to her strong character and lack of education, remained silent.

The ladies left, not entirely satisfied, but Maria was greatly relieved because she now knew Berni did love her—a doubt that had plagued her desperately in recent days.

Berni only learned of everything the next day, as he had been at a party.

Just 48 hours later, the phone rang at Maria's house, and on the other end was Berni. "Sorry, Maria. Please listen, don't hang up." Berni spoke from a long distance. "Forgive me, I admit my lack of seriousness. I love you, and as proof, I invite you to come to the city of Señora to become my wife. I've made all the arrangements at the church for our wedding."

Maria didn't say anything. She had started crying. "Al, Al," Berni called out, and Maria cried louder. She could sense that he was there. The emotion overwhelmed her.

Berni spoke to her like never before, with his heart in his words. He had told her he loved her before, but now his voice was more sincere and serious. "If you wish, you can come tomorrow, and we'll get married."

Maria could hardly believe it; it seemed like a dream. Just two days ago, Berni had left without saying goodbye, firmly stating "No," and now he was begging her to marry him and offering a church wedding. It couldn't be real. It simply couldn't be.

After an hour of conversation and promises from Berni, Maria woke up to reality and stopped crying. She told him to wait for her the next day at eleven in the morning at the taxi station in the same part of the city.

Berni arrived very early. From the car, he saw Maria descend. She looked more beautiful than ever, dressed elegantly and offering him a sweet smile.

They arrived at the church, where many people were waiting for them, though only Miryam, Berni's sister, her husband, and a few friends attended. The ceremony was intimate, and afterward, they went to a reception at Maria's sister's house before leaving for their honeymoon. They truly loved each other, and when there is love, passion follows naturally.

Berni returned to the Sultana. No one in the city knew that he had gotten married, not even his most recent conquest, a beautiful young woman barely 16 years old, with white skin, black eyes, a sensual mouth, a small, slender body, and such extraordinary charm that everyone adored her. She had just arrived from La Perla del Otún and started working at the same company where Berni had been employed for five years. In less than three months, she had Berni completely captivated by her smile, her gaze, and her elegance. Well, Berni would say with certainty when asked why he had so many girlfriends, that all women had something beautiful about them.

In the depths of his heart, he was honest. Esmeralda was the only one who knew that he had married, and they both agreed to keep it a secret to avoid gossip from their office colleagues and friends. This was mainly to ensure Esmeralda's family wouldn't oppose their continued friendship.

But a married man cannot act like a single man, and this caused Berni many problems. Despite his best efforts, he had to end the friendship. However, strange forces—forces of blood, care, and temptation— pulled at him. It seemed as though he were cursed by some serious incantations, bound by a spirit to return to someone or something. Once again, Berni found himself surrounded by girlfriends, friends, and lovers. The worst part was that everyone in the Sultana knew he was married, but this did not stop his sexual adventures, which only fueled his desires.

When he found it difficult to win the affection of a woman, he resorted to a trick that had always worked for him. He would say, "Believe me, my charming princess, I married just to give my last name to my daughter, so she would be born within a Catholic, legal marriage, before God and society. But her—referring to his wife, whom he loved immensely—I don't love. When you accept me, I'll take all the steps to get my divorce!" With these promises, he got what he wanted.

At other times, things were easier for him. When he was studying at university, he would leave his jacket on the back of his chair. After checking his clothes for the next day, he often found candy wrappers in his jacket pockets. He arrived at class, went up to the podium, and said, "The lady who put the candy wrappers in my jacket pocket can call my office tomorrow so we can have a friendly relationship. But if we understand each other, it might turn into a serious friendship. My phone number is 007-6969."

The next day, five classmates called, all claiming to have put the candy wrappers in Berni's jacket.

Berni was advancing economically at the insurance company. In addition to his salary as head of the motor vehicle department, he earned double in commissions from insurance sales. He was also part of the finance committee of a prominent coffee milling company in the city and worked as an advisor to an insurance company with offices abroad, for which he received a salary. This financial stability allowed him to enroll as a freshman at the university, where, within his first days, he made five friends—two of whom became true lovers. They adored him from the moment they had him between their tasks.

Once, there was a reception to inaugurate the "Paraiso" hotel in the city. Among the guests was the rector of the university Berni attended, the mayor of Sultana, Dr. Riascccifti, and other prominent personalities. Suddenly, they congratulated him and remarked, "It's incredible. You, Dr. Gomez, are the only one in the world and your nation, who manages to sit down in clear harmony for a conversation with your distinguished wife, your adorable girlfriend, and your sensual lover." Berni looked toward them and simply responded with a "Thank you, my respectable colleagues."

Berni, the son of Dona Carmelita and Don Marco, who had been exiled and erased from the list of Monseñor, the Apostolic Vicar of the Island—practically expelled from his friend's house under suspicion of having gonorrhea—was now the most famous student at the university. Early on, he gave a lecture on divine law and positive law. He spoke to a full assembly about the creation of Adam and Eve, their descendants, and their lives. At the same time, he spoke about positive law created by man, referencing Darwin's theory of the evolution of species. He boldly stated that humanity would have to accept in the future that we are a natural evolution of chromosomes, continuously improving to create a perfect society with no illnesses and longer life.

With these new theories, Berni gained the support of his peers. In the midst of his studies, a classmate invited him to direct a weekly Gazette, which lasted only as long as a priest blesses himself, as it was labeled a "blunder" by the university. After a private conference, the two students, one in law and the other in journalism, were ordered to stop the publication or face expulsion. The student council, of which Berni was a member, supported him in continuing the publications, but Berni refused, fearing it would divide the students.

Tensions were already noticeable between the ultraconservatives and the liberals. In a student meeting, he said, "We are the founders of this university in this city, and we must take care of our image to gain the support of local authorities in order to obtain a building."

At home, everything was harmonious and happy. His wife loved him and supported his many endeavors. Though he did not love her, as he often told other women, they had three children: the eldest daughter, Carmelita, named after her grandmother; Berni Jr.; and Alberta. They were admirable, and when they were together, they radiated distinction and kindness, traits often mentioned by others. His children already stood out as the best students in school.

Alberto would later, many years after, open the door to Miami police detectives when they arrived asking for Berni, as a suspect in the murder of his nephew, who at the time was also his beloved wife's lover.

Berni also advised a widow's insurance agency. She knew nothing about contract techniques or sales, and he did it because he remembered his mother, Dona Carmelita, and how she would rush to help widows with dignity back in the City of Miracles.

At this office, he met his future secretary. She was a sixteen-year-old girl with skin the color of African pearls, long black hair, a small mouth, honey-colored eyes, and a slim body light as a hare, as swift in her office work as she was in life. She had the intelligence of very few women. Later, when Berni became an executive with his own insurance firm and a team of lawyers, he hired her as his personal secretary.

Chapter 4
The Fall of Innocence

But one morning, as Berni was immersed in his daily work—liquidating and approving insurance indemnity payments—he received a call from his eldest brother, the anatomical tailor. His brother told him that their father had left the previous day for Cascajal Island but had not arrived. It had already been 24 hours since his departure. Don Marco was living in his son's house after quarreling with his beloved negrita, Dona Carmelita. According to what Berni knew, Don Marco had felt neglected by his wife, who had been absorbed in her grandchildren and daughter Lucía's affairs.

The entire family mobilized, searching all the police stations in both cities, hospitals, clinics, and distant relatives' homes where Don Marco might have sought refuge. However, this was unlikely, as he was always decisive in his actions. He had mentioned at his son's house that he would visit his other son, who no longer worked with the elite intelligence police group and had been living on the island, employed by the port authority. The search was conducted simultaneously, and after 72 hours, a body was discovered floating in the mighty Cauca River, near a bend marking the boundary of the Agricultural City. The body was that of Don Marco, the father of eleven children, whom his beloved negrita, Doña Carmelita, had raised with deep love, respect, and unwavering fidelity.

The body was immediately taken to the forensic doctor's table in La Sultana, and in less than five hours, it was returned to the family for burial. Arrangements were made in the city of Señora with the funeral agency and the San Antonio church, as the family was devout and active in Catholic matters. People came in droves, passing in front of the coffin, many weeping, for this was a distinguished and beloved family, always helping others. The pharmacy, which had been open to the public for many years, became the most trusted means for Doña Carmelita to continue helping those in need. Relatives and friends arrived from La Sultana, the Island, the City of Miracles, and even Bogotá, all with sincere intentions to offer their condolences. Even people from Lomitas and the United States, where her daughter Luzmila lived—the unfortunate one who had once been married to the wolf—came.

The crowd was so large that volunteers helped set up tents tied to the roofs of houses across the street, and tables and chairs were rented. Neighborhood ladies took turns preparing and serving food for the attendees. Bottles of aguardiente arrived at the tables like manna for the chosen people.

In one corner of the house, already drunk, sat Arge and Berni. They talked and bet on who could collect more women's phone numbers—with the only condition being that they could not be nieces. After a while, Berni asked his brother if he had any idea why their father had drowned, given that he had left for the island to visit their brother. Arge, in tears, told him: "Our father committed suicide."

"What are you saying?" Berni asked. "That can't be."

"Yes, brother," Arge replied. He was always Berni's most trusted sibling, especially after Berni had written him letters from exile following the scandal involving his niece—Arge's daughter. "Our father left a letter explaining his reasons and asking everyone's forgiveness for this decision."

"Forgiveness, you say?" Berni asked, shocked.

"Yes, brother. He asked for forgiveness from our mother, from you for the punishment he inflicted on you unjustly, from all of us, and even granted forgiveness to those who offended him. He explained that he didn't leave the house because he felt abandoned by our mother, but because she expelled him—just as she had expelled you. He wrote: what really happened is that he lifted his granddaughter in his arms and blew bubbles of air on her stomach to tickle her. At that moment, mother walked in and accused him of abusing the girl. She threw his clothes into the street and reproached him: 'If you have such vices, with what authority did you punish your son to exhaustion?'—referring to you, brother. She told him: 'With what authority did you cast out Gustavo, making yourself responsible for his death?' This is what he left written."

When Arge finished speaking, Berni buried his face in his hands, tears streaming down his face. After a long silence, he said: "Dear brother, this story leaves me confused and deeply saddened. You know how much I loved and still love our old man. I had long erased those bad moments from my memory, and above all, I had forgiven my father, you, and everyone involved in that matter with your dear daughter. And I know they forgave me too. You, more than anyone, know what really happened. Don't worry, forget about it; pass me the bottle, because while I was talking, you were drinking and almost finished it." They both cried, drank, and embraced.

"I feel such sorrow for my father," said Berni.

"I feel the same," said Arge. "But don't think you have much to complain about, dear brother, because as the youngest, you didn't fare so badly. If you ask brother Adro, he was almost killed by father. And sister Miryam also has another story."

"Tell me everything, brother."

"I will—but only if you send for another bottle."

"Of course, why not? Give me a minute and I'll make it appear."

He stood up, struggling not to fall, and gave money to a nephew who happened to be passing by, asking him to buy two bottles of aguardiente. When others saw the bottles in the nephew's hands, they asked who they were for, and he replied: "For my uncle." They followed him, and three beautiful women came along. They arrived, took Arge and Berni by the hands, and brought them to the group. They were welcomed with applause because the aguardiente was already scarce.

What had begun as a sad story of the deceased "monkey" turned into a reunion of poets and storytellers, with more than twenty people participating. Each took turns, displaying their talents. When it was Arge's turn, he paused and said: "Tonight I can write the saddest lines. Write, for example: 'The night is starry, and the stars are blue and shiver in the distance. The night wind revolves in the sky and sings. Tonight I can write the saddest lines. I loved him, and sometimes he loved me too. On nights like this, I held him in my arms...'" He could not continue; tears stopped him from finishing the most beautiful verse humanity knows, created by the marvelous poet Pablo Neruda.

Then they handed another cloth to Berni to dry his tears and urged him to perform one of his recitations that had made him famous among family and friends. He had once recited at the first fair of La Sultana to great success. But Berni excused himself, saying that with all the liquor he had drunk, he could not coordinate the verses. He tried with "Red Carnations," then "Brave Ones," and "The Overseer's Duel," but failed. Apologizing, he said: "I will console you instead with a story that goes like this: A young man returned from the university and asked his father if he knew about politics, because in class, the professor explained it, but he couldn't understand. So the father explained: In short, in our house, we are the nation. Your mother is the government who distributes goods and enforces orders. I am the capitalist class who brings money to buy what is needed. You, the daughter and the baby, are the future of this society. The maid, on the other hand, is the proletariat, the poor. The boy thanked his father and went to bed. At midnight, the baby's cry woke him, and he called his mother, but she didn't hear, she was deeply asleep. Then he went to the maid's room, but she didn't open. He peeked through the keyhole and saw his father on top of the maid. The next day, over coffee, he told his father: 'Now I understand politics perfectly. While the government sleeps, the future of the people eats shit and cries for lack of attention, and the capitalist class, taking advantage of the situation, spends its time screwing the working class from behind.'"

The audience burst into laughter, and more people joined the group. Berni had to repeat the same story until he finally fell asleep in his chair.

Only three hours later, Berni woke up. Arge had also recovered from his drunkenness; he had slept for about the same amount of time. They looked for each other and sat in another corner of one of the improvised halls. Berni returned to the subject: "Tell me everything you know about our father, brother. Whatever it may be, I will never forget it."

"Our father," said Arge, "had a problem with reacting violently to any fault of his children. He could never control himself. He was so honest, clean, faithful, and respectful that he always wanted his family to be the same way."

"That's true," Berni added.

"Well then," Arge continued, "when our brother Adalberto was only seven years old, he took five pesos from our mother's purse and hid them in front of the house, there in the City of Miracles. When mother noticed shortly after, she somehow found out that our little brother was the guilty one. She told him that father would punish him when he came home for lunch at noon. This happened at nine in the morning, but the boy was so terrified that by the time the church bells rang at noon, he had developed a fever. At exactly noon, Don Marco arrived, took him to the tree in front of the house, tied him up, and said that after lunch, he would return to hang him for being a thief. The child, overcome with terror, developed a fever so intense it was burning him alive. He called his little friends, gave them all his toys, and told them that his father was going to kill him for stealing from our mother. When he saw Don Marco coming, he fainted. They had to pick him up and rush him to the hospital because he was severely dehydrated."

"I can't believe it," said Berni. "I think you're exaggerating. My God, that can't be true!"

Arge, with a gravely serious tone, replied, "I lived through that horrible nightmare, little brother. All of us believed father would kill Adalbertito. You know how serious our old man was in all his matters."

"Yes, of course, I know that," Berni said. "But I don't believe father would have killed him. I can't accept that ending. The Lord, my God, would not allow such things."

Arge—who had studied theology for over five years at the Jesuit seminary in the Holy City before being expelled by an armed squad of the elite army unit at his parents' request—replied to Berni: "God is all-powerful in good, but not in evil. When people are doing good, God helps them, but when they are doing evil, God is not there, because that path is not the Lord's. And Jesus Christ told us, after walking it, 'I am the way and the life.'"

"Yes, that's right, brother. Have a drink. But it's also true that because of that example, none of us ever again took what wasn't ours. Isn't that so, dear Arge?"

"Yes, you said it. They are hard lessons, but never forgotten."

"Well then, my dear Berni, you are studying law. Do you agree with the death penalty?"

"No, sir, not at all," Berni replied. "If the death penalty were the remedy for delinquency or crime, it would have been enough with the first execution to solve the problem. But by now, they must already be sitting prisoner number 2,000 in the electric chair, and deaths in Europe and the United States are more violent every day."

"Then don't you think," said Arge, "that we need the death penalty here in Colombia?"

"No, my dear brother. What we need is more schools and universities, more sports, more love, and less idleness, liquor, and sex."

"By the way, Arge, how many beauties' phone numbers do you have?"

"Uh, I don't know. Let me see…" He began searching through his notebook.

The first rays of sunlight appeared on the horizon when their sister Lilia brought them a large cup of strong coffee, telling them it would help sober them up. They weren't drunk, but they had drunk too much.

Berni's mind became clearer as he took the opportunity to ask Arge if suicides could be saved. Arge answered that they could, as long as the person repented of their sins with all their heart at the moment of the act and offered their soul to God.

Berni got up from his chair and went to the kneeler at the foot of his father's coffin. He knelt, wept, and gave thanks to God, confident that his father had asked for proper forgiveness. He felt calmer, and his face reflected a little joy amidst the pain. He truly loved his father.

The last son of Doña Carmen and Don Marco went in search of his mother. He reached her side, sat down, and told her what his brother had said about salvation. Doña Carmen was not crying—no one knew if she had no tears left after weeping for her children, or if she was restrained by resentment toward her "monkey," whom she had loved as no other woman could have loved a man. She replied, "May God will it so."

Doña Carmen carried a wound in her heart that still had not healed. Three weeks before that fateful day, she had been in her son's house, speaking with her "monkey." In the midst of the family, she knelt and offered him apologies for everything that had happened, begging him to return to their home in the Señora City. To convince him, she offered him the keys to a new, furnished house where they could live the rest of their lives without the influence or company of anyone else. But this did not move Don Marco. Contrary to everyone's expectations, he told his wife—the woman he loved and still loved, the one who had given him eleven healthy, perfect children and raised them with devotion—that she could return the way she came. She insisted, crying, repeating that she could not forget him, that she loved him as always. All was in vain. Don Marco resolutely said no, and from that moment on, no earthly or divine power could change his mind.

After the burial ceremony ended, everyone returned to their homes, except for some of Doña Carmen's children who stayed with her for several more days. Among them was Berni. The next day, Berni got up very early, went to the kitchen, prepared coffee, and carrying two cups, went to his mother's room. Finding her awake, he sat beside her, handed her one of the cups, and, without asking how she had slept, told her: "Mother, you are the widow with the most dignity in the world." Doña Carmen broke into tears, and Berni embraced her tightly. "Mother, cry all you want," he said. And Doña Carmen cried for five continuous years. Berni left the following week.

Doña Carmen was very Catholic, deeply devoted to the Sacred Heart of Jesus. She could not sleep, thinking that her beloved "monkey" might be among those waiting to enter hell. Three weeks later, she went to the San Antonio church and waited for Father Ramírez. When he finished his duties, he went to meet the most respected lady of Señora City.

"But Señora Carmelita, it's you! Forgive me for making you wait," the priest said.

"Father, I need your help," said Doña Carmen. And immediately added: "My husband, as you knew, was a man of great faith, a very Catholic man. But my conscience torments me to think that he might not be saved in the end because of his suicide."

"Respected lady," the priest replied, "in Romans 10:13 it says: 'Everyone who calls on my name shall be saved.'"

Immediately, Doña Carmen's face lit up, and giving thanks to God and the priest, she hurriedly left the church, went home, and went straight to the Bible to read the verse. Every day she cried and read the same passage. Then she read John 10:9, Matthew 11:28, and day by day, she increased her reading until she had read the whole Bible—which, in her more than seventy years of life, she had never read more than a page of. In this way, she found relief from her pain, stopped feeling resentment, and was able to once again dedicate herself to caring for her widowed daughter and grandchildren. The drugstore business rose in sales, and prosperity returned to the family.

The Gómez children—Doña Carmen's sons—along with the rest of the family and friends, returned to their businesses and jobs. César, the eldest son, the anatomical tailor, already ran a very reputable tailoring shop, with clientele that included judges, clerks, lawyers, and others from those circles. Adalberto, once a respected member of Colombian Intelligence—who had once entered the Sultana hospital with an elite military assault squad to protect the doctor who operated on his brother Gustavo—had become a port magnate. A dozen speedboats were registered to his company to ferry tourists from the island to places like "Isla Alba," "Juan el Chaco," and "La Boca de Ana," on the Pacific Ocean, just a few miles from Cascajal Island. He was also the best harbor pilot in charge of anchoring incoming foreign cargo ships. He made only one mistake in his entire career at the port: one day, while guiding a 3,000-ton American-flagged ship to berth at the dock, the reverse thruster didn't respond to bring her alongside, and the ship drifted toward the edge. He ran and stuck out his leg to try to soften the blow. He was rushed to the hospital with a fracture, but the official report from the Port Captaincy stated that the pilot, thanks to his intelligence, had averted a greater tragedy.

Arge—the son who did not become Pope of the Catholics—was now another businessman. He owned a fleet of trucks that he sent daily to the cities of La Sultana and Bogotá with goods and baggage. Besides managing a major transport company, he cashed checks given to truck drivers after the bank had closed, in exchange for cash. He served as president of the Dolphins Club, the Sharks, and was even an active member of the Mermaids Club, where he was famous for his charm and generosity with money—he had an altruistic calling.

Doña Carmen's daughters could not complain about their economic situation either. Lucila—the beautiful young woman "given" to a nurse in exchange for his help when Gustavo was gravely ill in the Sultana hospital—was prospering with her pharmacy business, and she had added medical consulting rooms and a household cleaning-goods store. For several years, the store had been managed by her own brother Jaime, the same one who once threatened her with a revolver when she accused him of stealing from her. He was so brazen that he opened a similar business just two blocks away, selling the exact same items Lucila bought for her store. No one believed Lucila's claim that her brother Jaime was a thief, because they all knew the story of little Albertico, the boy Don Marco had almost hanged for stealing.

Another problem Lucila faced was that when a woman came to buy medicine at the pharmacy and happened to coincide with one of

Doña Carmen's rounds through the counters, if the woman lamented being a widow, Doña Carmen would order her daughter not to charge her because widows deserved special treatment. "But mother," Lucila would protest, "I can't avoid charging; I'll go bankrupt. Special treatment should be given by the local government." In the end, Doña Carmen would win, because she started crying—remembering the widows she had helped—until Lucila relented.

Luzmila had settled very successfully in Miami. She was the doll-like girl with blue eyes like her father's, who had once been deceived by a man fate put in her path, a man who became her road of bitterness. Only crucifixion was missing, for he subjected her to every abuse imaginable. With a kick to the abdomen, he caused her a miscarriage. That ended the tolerance Lucila had maintained out of love. She packed her bags and went to the United States. At that time, it was very difficult to obtain a visa to enter the country, and after many embassy appointments, she decided to fly to the Bahamas and then, in a small private plane, was taken to Miami. She repeated this entry four times, traveling back to bring each of her children, until she had them all in the U.S. The U.S. government knows nothing of this great exploit.

Without a doubt, the day the authorities learn of Doña Carmen's daughter's heroism, her statue will be placed in the Hall of Fame alongside great figures in the history of the United States, like the legendary George Washington Carver.

Luzmila—another martyr of a "Beauty and the Beast" marriage— built, through her personal effort, a peaceful future for her children. Soon, she had a cutting and sewing workshop with more than fifty sewing machines, where she gave work to relatives and friends who had just arrived and lacked work permits—those who hide or change addresses upon learning that a family member or friend from their country is arriving. It happened to her specifically: the day after she arrived—without clothes, money, or documents (for that is how borders are crossed by air, land, sea, or river)—she went to her mother's cousin's house in New York to present herself, and the cousin refused to take her in, offering every excuse. She left her on the street.

She did not become the first licensed prostitute in that country—though she likely would have been granted a license because she physically resembled an American—because she was Don Marco's daughter. Had he found out, God knows what would have happened. She had no inclination for that life anyway, for she remained divorced for the rest of her life and was never known to be with another man—not even a ghost, for by now any ghost would be a familiar one.

Miryam lived in La Sultana del Valle, where she arrived from the City of Miracles. There, she bought a house to live in with her children and her husband—another poorly polished gem like the infamous Hugo "the Wolf." He had one "virtue": he was more diplomatic in his wickedness. Fortunately, the transport company soon transferred him to work in the City of the Gate of the Sun, on the Caribbean coast in the north of the country. Doña Carmen's daughter graduated in cosmetology from a city school and, within a few months, opened a beauty salon. She worked from eight in the morning to eight at night. Her workday was grueling but necessary because her husband—whom she herself had informed was not the man of her dreams—did not send money for the children's needs. She had to shoulder the responsibility alone, and this would not change: in the future, it was always Miryam who paid the family, household, and business expenses.

After Gustavo—the one who died absurdly, though from drunkenness, in a motorcycle accident—came Jaime, who, after a while, would become the black bird of Don Marco Aurelio's household. "This is the rake of a son," his own siblings said.

Devout to the Sacred Heart of Jesus, Doña Carmen believed in the story of hell and purgatory that makes Catholics fear such threats, uttered by priests and pastors. The Holy Father never names those places because he knows they do not exist. But her son Jaime dragged her into hell itself without Doña Carmen ever leaving this earth. He began displaying his "merchant skills" by looting his sister Lucila's pharmacy. From one day to the next, Jaime opened a hardware/variety and medicine shop a few blocks from Lucila's pharmacy. His stock mirrored hers—goods from here, and the same from there.

81

Once, when his sister shouted "thief!" at him, Jaime went home, took a gun from his store's cash drawer, and came back to her shop. There was no cure for Jaime. Later, he would cause even more suffering and dishonor to his family. Further on, you will learn when, where, and how he arrived handcuffed at a "gringo" prison in Houston, Texas—the most feared fate for any Colombian.

The weapon was a .38 long-caliber revolver. Jaime arrived at his sister's shop and, seeing her from the doorway, aimed the revolver at her, intending to fire—but fortunately, Doña Carmen stepped in front of Lucila. When Jaime saw his mother, he repented and tucked the gun back into his waistband. He immediately vanished from the sight of his family and the customers present. A few days later, there appeared a lawsuit in the Circuit Court of Buga—the Señora City: Jaime Gómez vs. Lucila Gómez, seeking payment for labor benefits, bonuses, overtime, compensation for slander, defamation, moral suffering, and other costs, such as attorney's fees and court costs. He also asked the court to order Mrs. Lucila to publicly ask her brother's forgiveness for having called him a thief.

Marco Jr., the tenth child of Don Marco and Doña Carmen, would be the one—the only one—who would not cause his parents suffering. Quiet, humble, obedient, honest—but slow to think—slow at everything. He saw only as far as the tip of his nose, not from blindness but from lack of interest. His sister Lucila—who had more heart than merchandise in her shop—gifted him a house in Alto Bonito, in the Señora City of Buga. This young man had such luck—or was so blessed by the Lord Jesus Christ, who once said: "Blessed are the poor in spirit, for theirs is the kingdom of heaven."

Marco Jr. possessed one of the greatest riches: his family. His wife worked to cover household expenses, and his children loved him more than even his own sister Lucila, who had given him the house to live in with his wife and children. His three children—one boy and two girls—proved how much they loved their father when, one day, as noble feelings were being displaced by material interests, they went on a hunger strike against their mother in favor of their father.

Marcos the carpenter—calm, kind, and willing—honored his trade despite being a poor worker when it came to dealing with wood.

Despite all those good qualities, he cannot be called a faithful man. None of Doña Carmen's sons were faithful to their wives. They say the apple doesn't fall far from the tree, but these sons denied that adage, for Doña Carmen and her "monkey," her husband, were the most faithful couple of all time.

Lilia was Doña Carmen's last daughter, born eleven months before Berni, the youngest of all. The whole family acknowledged that she most resembled Doña Carmen in face and figure—though in other respects, not at all. She was slow, without aspirations or ambition. Her youth passed without anything special, and she married a man she thought she loved. But in time, after bearing him five children, she realized it was not him she loved, but someone else. She was always late for everything. She was so slow that she already recognized she loved another—but had yet to remember his name. She would be invited to a wedding and arrive when the couple already had their firstborn. She had no known profession, and like her paternal aunts, she would sit at a table to play cards and forget to get up and go to bed—spending day and night seated.

So carefree and uninterested was she that she traveled to the United States, and instead of working—like every immigrant does—she sat down to play cards. After Lilia was born, Berni, the last of the children, came into the home. All of them were perfect.

From the time the eldest were children, this family was much admired by the people and their neighbors. Their parents were always proud of them. Each had their own character, and no one was like the other—in nothing, well, almost nothing. Because when it came to chasing women, they were similar—whether single, married, widowed, or separated, there were no obstacles for them. Of course, they were very diplomatic—discreet and quiet in action— and this facilitated their conquests. And there were many.

Once, when they lived in the City of Miracles, they celebrated the October 12 festivities—Day of the Race and the city's founding. With the help of some ladies, Doña Carmen dressed all her children up: the older ones as married couples and the younger ones as their children. The uniqueness of the parade lay in the fact that half of the family was light-skinned and the other half dark-skinned, mixed among themselves—light-skinned with dark-skinned "children," and vice versa. The group was called "The Castañeda Family," a replica of another family that had arrived years earlier from Old Antioquia. That day, they won first prize in a single performance at the Country Club's celebration. From that day on, the Castañeda family was revived by the Gómez family as a living portrait.

From that event stems the fact that all of them could easily play the part of actors. Among them, you could see César, Adalberto, Arge, Miryam, Jaime, and Berni. César gave up liquor for love of his wife—and on his knees begged her to buy him a bottle, because love ought to be purified with aguardiente. Adalberto promised his wife every weekend that he would stop drinking, and she never left him because she was always waiting for that weekend. In one such theatrical act, César turned his performance into a tragic comedy. Many years after his death, no one could still understand why he ended his days that way. Each of Doña Carmen's children wrote a tragic page in the family history. No one knows what fatal destiny Doña Carmen had to live, nor why. She never went looking for a fortune-teller to lay out the cards or to "cleanse" her. She did not believe in fortune-tellers and refused to undress for those who perform "cleansings." When friends invited her to such consultations, she proudly answered, as a devotee of the Sacred Heart of Jesus: "Only Jesus knows the future, by divine grace."

Doña Carmen blamed herself for her fate because of the mistake of having left her beloved City of Miracles. She didn't remember that she had been forced by her husband to avoid a family tragedy. Her husband, "el Monito," had saved himself from being killed by the Liberals. For her, Cali was hell, though she still didn't know that Cali—the beautiful "Sultana of the Valley"—was called the Branch of Heaven. In truth, people don't live as happily even in Heaven: they eat deliciously, enjoy the climate and the wind, and people aren't dead. Everyone goes to work and school or university, enjoying fellowship and love for their neighbor. The wealth of its people is the family they love above all.

They had indeed fled from Armenia, the capital of Quindío (formerly a department of Caldas), out of fear of the Liberals who were roaming the streets hunting Conservatives to kill in revenge for the death of

Doctor Jorge Eliécer Gaitán, a candidate for the Presidency of the Republic of Colombia from the Liberal Party. Don Marco never allowed a Liberal to enter his house, and for that reason, his daughters were left without suitors, as the majority of Armenia's population were Liberals—yes, "reds," but the good kind, because evil has no political color.

In guerrilla movements, gangs, subversive groups, organized crime, terrorists, and others, they don't recruit only Liberals; all kinds of people become part of them—experienced or not—like the young boys they force into their ranks. No one asks those children which party they belong to. Nowadays, these criminal groups have both kinds in their ranks—Communists, Socialists, Liberals, Conservatives, Greens, Blues, or Whites. In the white-collar groups, it doesn't matter which party one serves; only their boundless ambition for power and wealth matters.

Berni was back in his university classes, having enrolled when the law faculty was inaugurated in La Sultana. To that end, he had to move quickly beforehand, reading the laws and the Constitution—or "Magna Carta," as Colombia's supreme law is called—so he arrived prepared for the interview with the distinguished founding lawyers of the city. Being prepared, the interview was easy to pass. That very day, the interviewer asked him who authored the book *Twenty Love Poems and a Song of Despair*, and Berni answered: "It was the Nobel laureate Pablo Neruda," and the doctor corrected him: "You should say 'is,'" to which Berni added: "Was, and I regret it, because today that great poet, born Neftalí Ricardo Reyes, a Chilean, has died—on September 23."

The temptation posed by his secretary—only 17 years old—he pushed aside by turning page after page in the works of Aristotle, Machiavelli, Voltaire, Marx, Engels, Mao, and many others. In a study workshop with several classmates, he easily obtained top marks in his courses.

Chapter 5
The Accident

Berni was too busy to indulge in his infidelities; women surrounded him, but he tried to ignore them. He was becoming a faithful man without intending to, and a good husband without realizing it. He was becoming a renowned student and appeared in Criminal Court with ease, like the best criminal lawyer. He was invited to participate in court for important cases of prisoners.

Berni wanted to understand why his parents—or rather his father—was a dyed-in-the-wool Conservative ("godo"). He wanted to master politics not only nationally but internationally. "What is a Christian-Democratic government? I have to know this," he told himself, sitting on the benches outside his university cloister.

Why did his friend, the priest named Camilo Torres—like the independence hero—join the ranks of M-19, if he was a Catholic, Apostolic, Roman, full of faith? Berni sought answers and read with a thirst for knowledge: books on philosophy, politics, law, introduction to jurisprudence, and social sciences.

Why does a president order the massacre of the very people who elected him, merely for taking to the streets in protest? Why do they order the assassination of a president just because his government is on the side of the people? Why does the candidate of the moment promise peace and, once elected, order war? Berni had to resolve all these questions.

His classmate—later a graduate lawyer—Doctor Rojas invited him to the offices of Doctor Carlos Holguín Sardi, already governor of Valle del Cauca, to join the Conservative Party, with the offer of being placed in the second slot with Dr. Rojas for a seat on the Cali City Council. Berni thanked them for the offer but did not accept a place on the council list for Cali, the Sultana of the Valley.

In the open forums organized at the Universidad Libre de Colombia, he spoke about the need to create a student board that would communicate with the government of each term in order to secure reforms to politics, the courts, and the laws. "We have to abolish the death penalty used by some countries, because it serves no purpose. In the United States, for example, they execute a prisoner after he has spent a lifetime in prison, and the homicide and murder rate does not decline. We must advocate constitutional reforms to end fanaticism between parties, because it is a fanatic who causes the death of a candidate. A religious fanatic is the one who orders the death of others who do not share his religion or creed. Let us remember," he said, "the extermination of Christians at the hands of Catholic fanatics in the sixteenth-century Church, and also Christians against Catholics. On the other hand, there are crimes by sports fanatics who kill someone in a stadium because their team loses the match. We must get governments to solve these problems."

The students met and created a student council. Berni was appointed a member of the student council at the Universidad Libre de Colombia in Cali.

Many years later, when he had a column in the *Nuevo Herald*, Berni wrote an article titled "Testimony of a Fanatic," dated October 19, 1994. In the article, he explained that fanaticism is a blind passion, a deaf feeling born from belief, opinion, or dogma, which accepts no questioning or discernment from others. He cited other famous fanatics such as Pablo Escobar and Al Capone, who were fanatics of money.

Years later, Berni wrote letters to U.S. presidents, asking them to make the reforms necessary for good government. He received reply letters from well-known figures such as Bill Clinton (October 14, 1994), Barack Obama (June 17, 2013), and the famous Donald Trump (August 4, 2025). To the latter, he sent a proposal for immigration reform in the name of the American people. Berni, like his father Don Marco Aurelio, did not beat around the bush.

By this time, Berni was already in his fourth year of law school and working diligently in his legal practice. He presented a well-decorated law office to the public and his future clients, sharing the office space with other legal professionals.

One afternoon, a distinguished lady came to his office, her face reflecting anguish and confusion. She introduced herself and explained that three days earlier, she had lost her beloved husband. She wanted him to handle the probate action and liquidation of the marital assets. Berni immediately thought of his mother and, explaining that he had a legal clinic but could not yet practice, offered to help until the case was finished. However, it would require the signature of a licensed attorney. She raised no objection and was very grateful. She then showed him the documents she had: promissory notes, titles to two coal mines, deeds to buildings and houses, motor vehicle papers, account statements, bank notes, and many other records. While this was going on, Berni served her a soda, but the lady asked if he had any liquor because she was very nervous. Berni served her a brandy and a glass of milk.

"Drink it and try to relax, ma'am," he said. "Everything here is very clear and in order. I see no obstacle to a swift filing so you can begin to enjoy all your assets."

"I have great confidence in you and have heard very good things about your work," she said.

Berni stood up, came closer, took her hand, and kissed it, thanking her for her words. In that instant, he turned her hand over and, looking at her palm, said softly, "Your palm is very clearly marked. It can be read easily. Here is your future, your past, your life, your loves."

Mrs. Adais Arango, with a coquettish smile on her lips, asked, "Do you also know palmistry?"

"Oh yes, my respected lady," Berni replied. "In your soft and beautiful hands, I can read the heart's emotions, your happy loves, your great intelligence, your life. In this profession, one studies Plato, Socrates, Aristotle, and others who accepted in philosophy the influence of the stars on people's lives."

"Please read everything it says there," the lady said excitedly.

"Well, this line shows that your life will be long, and the greatest setback you've just passed. You will meet very important and famous people. You will easily resolve some unclear problems, apparently with siblings or employees. The line of love shows several, but one very special and passionate one that seems short, and another love that is longer, serious, and lasting."

She listened attentively. Berni looked into her eyes and saw her anxiety and excitement. He poured her another brandy, but she asked him to join her in a toast. He continued, "It may be that you will have more children, and the two you now have will be very happy."

The telephone rang, and Berni got up to answer. Mrs. Arango was astonished at what she had heard and, rubbing her face, said, "How wonderful. What you say is true. Doctor, I need you to keep reading my hands, but it is time for me to go to the mine to close up."

"Do not worry, we can continue another day," Berni answered.

"No, please, it must be today. Come with me to the mine, we will close, then we will go to my house and I will invite you for a drink."

They left together, arrived at the mine where several employees were waiting, and she handed over the keys to close. On the way back, she told Berni to take her somewhere quiet, because at her house there might be people waiting to offer their condolences for her husband's death. Berni was pleased to accompany her and, along the way, remembered his mother saying that helping a widow is worth more than helping three other people.

Each drove their own car and parked at a wooded spot within the city, in the south of La Sultana. The spot was simply beautiful, with trees and tropical plants not seen anywhere else. Couples went there to talk about their fate and their future. Each little hut was strategically located so that one could not see the occupants of another, nor hear their conversation. The music was ambient, leaving room for natural sounds and the birds' songs. Berni turned on the radiophone and ordered a bottle of aguardiente "with all the trimmings," he added, telling the man who answered. Berni continued reading her palms, and between bits of news and questions, they had one drink, then another, and another.

A while later, they had lost track of time. They began their romance and, between kiss and kiss, drifted through the corners where only lovers, hungry for passion and sex, arrive. They didn't realize when one of the legends on the line of love was being fulfilled. People resemble the land where they live, and indeed this woman was as beautiful as a diamond yet unpolished. Only the heat of Berni's passion, at 900 degrees Celsius, could melt her.

Three days later, the respectable and distinguished lady was calling again to request a new appointment.

Berni, the best student of his period at the university, would study a case, and immediately, the alibi that would save the defendant would come to mind. Then, before the jury, he would use all his craft to argue within the same case, without stepping outside the parameters of the alleged crime, the necessary grounds to convince the jury that his client was not responsible for what was charged.

The day after touring the coal mines with the widow, another lady was chasing him and calling out for him to wait. He noticed and stopped. There, in front of the Bolívar Theater, the woman hugged him and planted a kiss on him. Doctor Gómez could do nothing to avoid it because of the surprise of the act.

"Please tell me, ma'am, to what do I owe such an expressive and pleasant greeting?" he asked.

She replied, "Doctor, you saved my son from the prison where he had been for two years. My offspring, in fact, my only child, is free today thanks to God and to you."

"Who are you talking about, ma'am? What is your name?" he asked.

"My name is Digna Romero. I am a widow and the mother of Aristóbulo Romero, the young man you defended in court," she said, adding, "I have no way to pay your services, but I will be eternally grateful."

"Ma'am, you owe me nothing. Give my regards to your son," he said.

Berni's fate was sealed. Widows sought him out like bees to pollen.

The doctor returned to his office and began to recall the case. At the Meléndez resort, on the bank of the river of the same name, a very serious tragedy had occurred about two years earlier. A young man had arrived there with his girlfriend and his mother in search of a bit of leisure. When he went to find the kitchen of the place, he had to cross a long stretch. Midway, in the middle of the dance floor, a man came staggering toward him, carrying a tray full of empanadas. He bumped into the other, and the empanadas fell to the floor. The offended man insulted him, shouting "son of a bitch" at the young man who had arrived only five minutes earlier. The young man apologized and said he would order another round, but the enraged drunk lunged at him and, since he was drunk, they both rolled on the floor. In the struggle, bottles fell and shattered to pieces. After a few minutes, perhaps five, one of them stood up, but the other—the one who wanted to resolve the incident with fists—could not get up. "Leave him there, he's drunk," some said. "He's playing dumb," others shouted. The man never managed to stand. He bled out from a severed artery. The other could not even sit down, because after leaving his companions at the table, he left in search of his fate. The next day, he was charged with first-degree murder. He was facing a sentence of 25 to 40 years when Doctor Gómez took charge of his defense.

He also remembered telling the jurors the following: "Honorable and respectable members of this jury, the event that brings us to this court today proves once again that we, that is, you, the government, society, and I, are the ones truly responsible for the matter before us. The accused is innocent, and we should be the ones on trial. My client is yet another victim of the failure to educate our fellow citizens. I am convinced, as you will be at the end of my statement, that if we take everyone to school, these lamentable cases will not occur, or we will not have to live through them in our society. Surely nothing would have happened if these events had occurred in one of our city's clubs, San Fernando, or Club Colombia, to name a few, where educated and cultured people meet. The same has happened in those places, but there is no death. Those involved apologize, then go together to the kitchen to repeat the order, and perhaps the responsible party pays for it, but they never resort to violence, and certainly not to the tragic result of the death of that young man, José María Morates. He was a man who got drunk and, once intoxicated, threatened those present wherever he happened to be. Witnesses say he always seemed dangerous. He was one of those who, as the poem says, 'brave men who drink their cups and splash them with blood; brave enough to make a body a husk, but bitter for work in the furrow, for rising at dawn.' All that machismo, that disposition for fighting, drugs, drunkenness, and the rest, stemmed only from the fact that such individuals did not attend school. That is the responsibility of parents, society, and the government."

"The Constitution of Colombia, the most beautiful charter of law ever birthed by human intelligence, states that every Colombian is entitled to free education. Of course, we provide elementary education, but secondary and university education must be paid for, and many cannot afford it. The result is an immense majority of young people crowding the labor force, and some overcrowding the prisons in the best cases, because the rest, unfortunately, end up in cemeteries. How sorry I feel for that victim and for those who at this very moment are headed to their final resting places; how sorry I feel for that young man who sits there awaiting your wise decision to declare him innocent. How sorry I feel for those mothers, because both were mothers of an only son. Coincidentally, the accused is an only son and supported his family, while the victim, too, was an only son, but in his case, his mother supported him. He was a known idler, familiar to the authorities in his neighborhood. But his unfortunate mother will never stop mourning him day after day because of that."

The defense spokesman, the law and criminology student, the son of Doña Carmen, added, "The protagonists of the event before us were not carrying weapons at the moment of the incident, nor before, as the witnesses say. This was an unfortunate and tragic accident. Yes, one died, but it could have been the accused. The deceased died

92

because he lost all his blood from the cut he suffered from one of the many bottle shards that were scattered on the floor. None of the witnesses saw the defendant holding anything in his hands—nothing resembling a knife, bottle, or piece of glass."

Doctor Gómez asked the jury to declare his client innocent, as he had acted in legitimate defense of his life.

It was the young man's mother who ran after him in the street to tell him that God would repay him for having won her son's freedom, and she gave him a grateful kiss.

Doña Carmen's children were relocating. These adjustments become necessary as their children grow up. Some moved elsewhere to improve their income, others to strengthen their networks of friends, and the rest were obliged to move for work or transfers—sometimes to pursue university studies.

The only one who never changed address was the eldest, the anatomical tailor. From the day he married, he went to live in the Sultana of the Valley, in the same house, the same bed, and the same chair he used to sit in to sew. He placed that chair at the shop's front entrance for fifty straight years without missing a day, from seven in the morning to seven at night. He didn't persist out of love for work, but out of love for gossip. With his sweet, friendly greeting, he would make anyone passing by stop, and with the tricks of a great performer, he drew out all the information he wanted to know. Neither the mayor nor the local inspector could know as much about the people and the city as César.

The others had already changed residence. Adalberto returned to the City of Miracles after being put on disability by the port after colon surgery that left him with a colostomy—which he jokingly called a "colon-tomy." He kept living there, watching his neighbors' children grow, because he had thrown his own children out into the street when they were still almost kids. He had less patience than his father—who had once waited until noon to hang him from a tree for stealing from his mother, but forgave him when he fainted. Adalberto wouldn't let his children back into the house, simply because the eldest was a drug addict, the second an alcoholic, and the girl showed a tendency toward lesbianism. People said what was happening to him was God's punishment. "Blessed be the ignorance of some people," Berni would reply—that it was less a punishment from God than the harm he himself inflicted on Olga, and why should she suffer it, since she was the kindest, most saintly woman in the region? His wife, Olga—the children's mother—had always been a good mother, after being a good daughter, and the best wife. She devoted herself full-time to caring for her husband after his surgery for rectal colon cancer. She knew that her beloved "little stump," as she always called him, would never again be able to have sexual relations with her. She ended up deaf, but that problem did not keep her from hearing the word of God. She converted to Christianity.

Argemiro moved to the Capital of Music, Ibagué. His children studied at the city's best schools and were well-equipped to enter university through the front door. But destiny had greater suffering in store for him because of one of his children, who, as his sister would later experience, went through a crisis. Some years later, that beloved son would cause him the greatest grief of all. Then he moved back to the Sultana and later to Cascajal Island, always with his children—he only separated from them to go to the bathroom.

Lucila was doing well financially, thanks to the profitability of her pharmacy. It had the best stock in the area and offered the best service.

In the United States, Luzmila was happy, but she began to notice that her sons—"the Chinese" and Hernán—came and went from New York, carried money and weapons, and held private but important meetings with "friends." This worried her deeply, and she couldn't understand why people said they were involved in the drug business. "It's unfair for the family to say that about them," she would insist. Like each of Doña Carmen's children—and of the now-deceased Don Marco—Luzmila would suffer a grave tragedy with her two sons that left a wound in her heart for the rest of her life.

Another daughter, named Libertad, moved back to the City of Miracles the day after her mother died. She and her husband raised their beloved children there. They won a ticket in an Official Lottery in the Sultana—being the only ones to gain anything from that "damned city," as Doña Carmen called it when she heard the news. Her resentment came from having gone, in her anguish to save her son Gustavo's life, from church to church seeking the Sacred Heart of Jesus—and not finding it. Besides, in the City of Miracles, she was Doña Carmen, known and loved by the entire society—from the most diehard Liberal to the most distinguished Conservative, from the mayor to the newest station inspector, from the baker to the worst butcher, from the bishop to the parish priest. In the Sultana, she was just "the lady on the corner."

Lilia—the girl-woman who married a man as charming as he was poor—was pushing her children forward in school, while her husband worked at full capacity for an appliance distribution company, from which he was later fired for having violated the moral standards and good customs of the Japanese (firm/community). Jaime ran his notions shop and competed with his own sister just 300 meters from Lucila the widow's pharmacy. Jaime got better discounts on merchandise because he went out drinking with the sales reps from Droguería Humanitaria, whereas his sister couldn't even allow the salesmen to take her hand, because there was Doña Carmen's watchful eye repeating, "They only show you love for the money you have." Lucila knew that was partly true, but it was also true that it had been more than twenty years since her last sexual encounter with her husband—two weeks before he died, in fact—because the fool worked double shifts, and when his wife returned from her perfumed bath, ready for intimacy, her man lay in bed like a corpse.

Aurelio was Doña Carmen's beloved son—but not because he was the best son, because none of them were. Rather, he was slow to think, slow to decide, and slow to act. He never looked beyond the tip of his nose—not from blindness, but from lack of initiative. A born carpenter, yet a poor worker when it came to wood. Nevertheless, compared to many of his neighbors, he was the most honest and hardworking. He had four wonderful children, very humble and of good will. His children are in the Guinness Book of World Records for being the ones who loved their father the most— no one has ever offered, nor will ever offer, such love to a father as they did. One of the many pieces of evidence to support this is that when their mother threw his suitcase and clothes out into the street and changed the door locks so he couldn't come into his own house

95

at dinnertime, the children would go on hunger strike and leave the food on the table, declaring they would not take a single bite until their father was invited back in. They didn't do this just once, but as many times as their mother tossed his things into the street. And the most striking thing is that they always knew their father's expulsion was due to his own irresponsibility—the beloved son of Doña Carmen. Those hunger strikes included a sea of tears shed by all of them.

This case became well-known and widely talked about, and people said that Aurelio's wife was the only one who allowed herself the luxury of closing the door on her husband—because the other daughters-in-law of Doña Carmen, on the contrary, closed their doors to keep their husbands from going out. "I hope," said Doña Carmen, "that it never occurs to Dalilita, Noelia, Olguita, or María Eugenia to throw my sons out, because they won't come back."

Berni, the youngest—the "boy," as Doña Carmen called him—was at the peak of his powers. He worked, studied, danced, held business meetings; he came and went, fulfilling every commitment—to everyone, and especially to his lady friends. He was outstanding in his social life. It was hard to understand how he also managed his home and children: three precious offspring, flawless in their studies, their games, and their wholesome adventures. They were very happy children—and their parents too. But one day, while they were all seated at the table eating together, Berni noticed something strange in his son Berni Junior's right eye.

"Wait, son, wait," he said. "Please look very slowly to the left—yes, like that. Now back to the other side, slowly." (It was like the exam of the world's best ophthalmologist.) "Upward, then downward. Good, son, thank you very much." He rose from the table and went to his room to cry. His wife followed him and, closing the door behind her, reached him and asked what was wrong. Berni told her that their son showed a strange mass in his eye and that they had to take him to the doctor the next day. She could say no more; she burst into tears, and they embraced. The children finished eating with the housemaid and then went out to play. "How can our son have that in his eye?" Berni wondered, and held his wife back from bringing the boy for another exam. "Tomorrow we'll take him to the city's best ophthalmologist—Doctor Cuartas will surely see him. Don't cry anymore," he said, trying to console her.

At dawn, Berni got up. He and his wife hadn't slept a single minute. At seven in the morning of the new day, they left with their five-year-old son for Dr. Cuartas's clinic. The doctor called them aside and gave them the news: "The boy has a convergent retinoblastoma in his right eye. He will lose the eye in a little less than thirty days," he added, in words as grave as the disease. "I'm very sorry." In a few choked words, he told them to bring the boy back the next day for further tests. "In any case, you are free to take him to another specialist so you can be sure of my diagnosis." They didn't hear the rest, because the pain had broken their hearts. They stood there against the wall, holding their son, who also cried without understanding. Then they left the clinic.

In their car, down a street they didn't know, in a place they didn't know, they could barely make out people they didn't know. They looked but did not see—just like their son.

After five hours—by midday that same day—they walked through the doors of Dr. Fernández's clinic, a Spaniard with a reputation as a skilled ophthalmologist. He told them the same thing. Three days later, they were coming down the stairs of the plane that took them to Bogotá, and an hour after that, they were entering the Barraquer Clinic, the best eye-diagnostic center in all of the Americas. While they waited, they met dozens of cases like their son's and twice as many people who had come from every corner of the world. This clinic was famous because its professionals had trained at the same clinic in Spain, already renowned for its procedures. Berni asked a Spaniard why he was there if his country had an identical clinic, and the man answered that here it was more affordable for his means. That afternoon, they left with the same diagnosis as before. The only new thing was that they were offered a connection to the city of Medellín to order a prosthesis.

Desolate, they found themselves in a place they had never imagined being. Sitting on a bench in a small garden, they watched as little birds picked food off the ground and carried it to their chicks in the nest. Suddenly, María—Berni's wife—remembered that someone had recommended visiting the Virgin of Chiquinquirá, patroness of Colombians. "She's very miraculous," she said. "Yes, of course—let's go see," Berni replied. They took a taxi and begged the driver to take them to the Virgin's church. They crossed nearly all of Bogotá and then a road to arrive there. They went in and knelt before Her Majesty, the Divine Virgin of Chiquinquirá. They had never seen her, though they had heard of her.

After returning to the Sultana, a friend recommended to Berni that when it comes to the eyes, the Virgin who could work the miracle of curing their son was Saint Lucy—the most miraculous one was in Medellín. They bought the tickets and, the following week, were there with little Berni, prostrate at Saint Lucy's feet—beautiful, miraculous, grand. Berni's parents already knew the prayer by heart; on the flight, they had learned it from beginning to end, letter by small letter.

They came back, then set out again. They went wherever anyone told them to go. They were desperately seeking a miracle. "My God!" Berni exclaimed. "But I already have the one who will work the miracle." He told his wife one night as they were talking about it. She sat up in bed and asked, "Then say it already, please! Who?" "The Sacred Heart of Jesus. How foolish I've been—no one else can do it, I'm sure," Berni answered.

They set out at sunrise with their son and went to the Church of the Sacred Heart of Jesus. Once there, they knelt before the image and, praying in silence—without having planned it—they begged the Lord for their son's health. An hour later, they were confused, repeating the same words and drinking their own tears. The mother leaned over to look at her little one and found him asleep. The boy lay there in all his beautiful innocence. With her mouth closed, María said: "My Father, I offer you my eyes—or if that is too little, I offer you my life—in exchange for my son's sight, or better, for your son's sight, for he is yours and I have him as your blessing; but I know that one day I must return him to you. Meanwhile, please grant him a way to see." During morning Mass, just as she came back to herself, the priest, speaking of the word of God, said: "If your eye causes you to stumble, pluck it out. It is better to enter the Kingdom of God with one eye than, having two eyes, to be cast into hell."

María lowered her head and asked God's forgiveness for her lack of humility. She looked at her husband, and he was looking at her; they embraced and wept without hearing the final words of the sermon. They left the church just as they had left Dr. Cuartas's office the first day: completely unmoored, with a pain in their hearts that bordered on a heart attack.

Once they had read the passages of what Jesus said, according to Mark 9:43, Berni Jr.'s parents found a little peace. Peace? With their beloved son only ten days away from losing his eye? Something more had to be done, Berni told himself every day, and he told people what was happening to him. When the news reached the ears of a friend's wife, she called him, and they met to talk. It was about a "medium"—someone who mediated with good spirits to heal people, but it was essential that the person have faith.

Berni agreed, and the next day they went in search of the man who acted as the go-between.

When Berni confessed to the man that he didn't have much faith in spirits, only in the Sacred Heart of Jesus, the man told him that was enough. The session was tremendous. The medium was transformed and, in the midst of a trembling that seemed to bring the walls down, began to circle around the boy—who was standing in the middle of a bright room, it was mid-afternoon—and, raising his arms above his head, he whirled his hands and spoke in other tongues (Berni half-understood it to be ordinary German) and then intoned Latin. About fifteen minutes passed, but when the man began to calm his shaking, he recovered his usual speech and, sweating profusely, told Berni he had not achieved anything. "But follow these instructions to the letter," the miracle-worker insisted. "Go home and arrange the boy's room, leaving only his bed; a table; a washbasin and a pitcher, both aluminum; a clean towel; two packs of gauze; alcohol; and some cotton. The curtain, the towel, and the sheet must be white. So must the cloth that will cover the table. No one else may be in the room. Tonight, the boy will be operated on by Doctor Gregorio Hernández, an ophthalmologist who practiced in Venezuela some years ago. In spirit, he has told me he will visit tonight, in your very house." Berni promised—without believing the slightest bit—that everything would be arranged exactly as requested. He asked how much he owed, and the man said nothing; that after the operation, if he wished, he could bring or send a donation. Berni left the room and, despite what the medium had said, went to the receptionist and left enough money so as not to be forgotten.

At home, he told his wife in detail not only about the session but also the neighbor's instructions. "But you were in the same room with them?" María asked. "Yes, yes, of course—I watched his every move. It was extraordinary, but I think because of my little faith in such people, we didn't manage to attract the spirits' visit." "All right," the boy's mother added. "I'll arrange everything to await Saint Gregorio's visit."

Hope took hold of María, and filled with blind faith—in God, in Jesus, in the Holy Spirit, in Gregorio Hernández, in Peter, Paul, Hyacinth, and Joseph—she lay down without sleeping, awaiting her son's groans. Berni didn't sleep either, but he didn't speak. At dawn, sleep finally overcame them. Sunbeams entered through the window and woke them. They closed and opened their eyes, got up, went to see their son, opened the door—and there he was, asleep. On the floor lay gauze stained with fresh blood, cotton wet with alcohol, and the towel—slightly wrinkled but clean. The water in the pitcher was lower, and there was a little clean water in the washbasin. Then they looked at the pillow; it was stained with a yellowish, foul-smelling liquid. The little eye was closed, with a bit of residue that could have been discharge. The boy slept deeply. They embraced and began to cry, covering their faces with the ends of the towel. They couldn't believe it—or, now, they believed, but didn't understand. Many years later, they still didn't understand, even less when they looked at their son's eye—by then, the boy was a 33-year-old man.

Berni Jr. did not regain sight in that eye, but his parents came to think that to enter the Kingdom of God, it was not necessary to see with both eyes.

Berni personally went to deliver a large donation to the man he had once visited, whom at first sight he had thought wouldn't be capable of carrying even the salt for lunch.

Berni and his family recovered quickly from all they had suffered—a suffering that pierced their hearts and shattered their daily life. The drama rippled into other families, such as those of their parents, siblings, and even their friends' homes.

He recovered at the university as well and returned to the insurance companies' cocktail parties, where he was a special guest. He learned that the university was preparing for the graduation of the first cohort—the founders—because the six-year education reform for law students had not caught up with them. The ladies would take care of the rings and reception; others went looking for the venue; and Berni, with his elite group, was to secure the funding, the orchestra, the liquor, and the food. Of course, the menu had already been chosen.

Soon—barely ten months—Berni would be one of the most respected lawyers in the country: not only for his honesty, but for his intelligence and heart. His specialty would be criminal and civil law, based on Roman law and the Chilean code. He was an expert in the theories of the born criminal, the converted one, and the repentant. In civil matters, he came to draft the perfect complaint—even while still a practicing student.

But fate had set a miserable trap for him, and its bearer was the last person the brilliant, soon-to-graduate student would have imagined.

It was a beautiful Friday afternoon—"cultural Friday," as some called it; later, they would call them "socials" to make them sound more democratic. Executives, lawyers, and employees moved to secure cash or an increase in available balance on their credit cards. Through the manager, the bank granted a line of overdraft to the account holder, with the promise of covering it before month-end or the monthly close. That was the day's most important business. After ensuring the money for his wife's purchases, Berni managed a surplus to celebrate the weekend. For this, a single phone call to one of his girlfriends—or lovers—was enough; then he would sit and wait to go out.

Chapter 6
Broken Dreams

Berni looked at the clock and decided to leave the office thirty minutes after four in the afternoon. He took a book from his library and opened it to page 66. At the top of the page, it read: "The Crisis of the West."

The secretary came into his office and announced a visit from Doctor Rudolf Mandarino, one of the city's most prestigious attorneys and Berni's professor for Civil Law. Berni stood, shook his hand, and—with all the respect due a teacher and his customary warmth—invited him to sit and immediately asked what he'd like to drink. Berni kept fine liquors, milk, water, tea, and coffee in his office. The professor accepted only a coffee. After the usual greetings and small talk, Doctor Mandarino got to the point.

"Doctor Berni," he said, "the reason I'm visiting you today is that you have a lawsuit against Mr. Justino Laverdez. This money"—he set a check on the desk—"should come in handy on a Friday like today, and it represents your fees for that lawsuit. I expect that tomorrow, Saturday, you will be at the courthouse first thing to file a notice of withdrawal, request the lifting of the provisional measures, and arrange the delivery of the vehicle (a 40-ton tractor-trailer) to my client. I'm sorry to leave so quickly, but I have other matters waiting at my office." Doctor Mandarino stood up.

"Your honor, please don't go. Give me a few minutes to calculate the claim, because my fees are irrelevant and not collectible—I'm still a trainee. The principal, interest, and court costs, however, are of utmost importance to me and to my client. At least, that's what you yourself, my respected professor, taught me."

"Take it or leave it, Doctor," he replied. "Because the truth is, I can have that vehicle back on the road tomorrow, or Monday at the latest. You'll see, once you face reality, that what counts is what you have in your hand—and today I'm offering fabulous fees for a student like you. As for your client—forget him."

"Forgive me, Doctor," Berni said. "I can't withdraw. I'm not going to—today, tomorrow, or ever. I'll do so only when the total amount of the judgment is deposited in the Popular Bank. After that, I will certainly deliver the trailer and tractor to whomever you indicate. Allow me to add something"—Doctor Mandarino listened with a mocking smirk—"First, I am the son of Marco Gómez, the most honest man who ever lived on this planet. Second, my client expects the best service from me—he told me so right in that very chair you're sitting in. Third, when I listened to your lectures, you taught me how to recover an unpaid debt, and at no time did you mention that a civil case in court should end the way you're proposing. I'm very sorry not to oblige you. Take your check off my desk. You may go."

The professor took the check, stood up, and pronounced this verdict: "Berni, it's one thing to be a good academic and another to be a practicing lawyer. You'll be lawyering your way to ruin if you continue with this romanticism. You're losing a fine chance to earn your first, well-deserved fees. I assure you: on Monday I'll be getting that vehicle out of the impound lot. I will file the necessary documents for its return. Good day, Doctor." With that, the lawyer-professor left.

On Monday, Berni went early to the judge's chambers to report what had happened with the defendant's attorney. The judge asked his clerk for the file, and—to Berni's astonishment—the release orders had already been issued, and the written notice to the motor-vehicle yard authorities requesting delivery had been sent. The tractor-trailer had been released from attachment.

In the record, there appeared a title of ownership dated one year before the lawsuit, with notarized entries, signatures, and national stamp-tax payments all duly legalized. It was a forged document, crafted with sufficient formal trappings to pass as valid evidence before the court. The judicial steps had been carried out since the previous Saturday. A fraudulent maneuver—astonishingly "legitimate."

Berni was stunned. In the same file, there was another title dated only three months earlier, issued by the motor-vehicle registry naming the defendant as owner.

Dr. Berni Gómez—son of Doña Carmen and Don Marco, the top student of Colombia's most renowned law school—was left with no legal ground to stand on as he made his way back to the university.

That same Monday, Berni went to a shop that sold only aguardiente and sat down as he ordered a bottle. His head was spinning. He remembered his Introduction to Law professor speaking about ethics, morals, and the vocation for the profession—respect for the law. Doctor Quijano Yacup repeated these lessons every time he began his classes. Berni downed one drink after another, muttering to himself that he didn't understand. Hours passed, and after three, he felt as if a tractor-trailer loaded with 50 tons had run over him, crushing him under its weight.

The next day, he arrived at his office and, like a madman, rummaged through his desk, tossing papers everywhere. Suddenly, he grabbed something in his hands, raised his arm, put it in front of his face, and stared at it. Then, with a clenched fist, he threw the object into the trash basket. It was his graduation ring.

That day, Doctor Berni Gómez swore he would never be sworn in as a lawyer.

The following day, Berni drew up a complete list of the legal matters he had underway in the city courts—civil and criminal cases—and began substituting other attorneys one by one as counsel of record. He sent his clients the documents he held and stored, at his wife's parents' house, all the diplomas he had earned at other universities, including a criminology degree from the University of Santiago (founders' cohort). He also filed away his high-school diploma from the Colombian Institute of Higher Education in Bogotá. Nostalgia overwhelmed him when he remembered that in only six months, he had achieved the ICFES graduation score—a feat that usually takes seven years. He had shut himself in his office every day, and many nights, studying until he achieved "401 points out of the 400 required," as he liked to say.

His university classmates tried to help and get him to return, but Berni wouldn't listen to reason. He devoted himself to drink and poker, and every day, he and three friends would go to one friend's country house, where they played and chatted late into the night. Tipsy on aguardiente, he would recite that a son of Don Marcos Gómez could never be a lawyer or politician, because Don Marcos was an exceedingly honest man. Many people sidled up to whisper in his ear, offering "special services," but Berni would tell them no. At that time, contract killings by hired assassins called "parrilleros" were in vogue—masked men on motorcycles who killed, often using a woman's stocking to cover their faces. Identifying these hired criminals was nearly impossible, and although some suspects were detained after crashing during their escape, no one could point them out in a lineup because no one had seen their faces.

But then Doctor Rudolf Mandarino collapsed at his doorway while trying to open it. At the university hospital morgue, they found five bullets in his body, which had caused his death almost instantly.

Berni went to his former professor's house and, asking for Doctor Mandarino's brother, offered his condolences. Hugging him tightly, he whispered in his ear: "I'm with you in this hard moment. Remember we're all in transit to a better place. If you need any help of any kind, let me know; I'm here to serve you." Then he left. Doctor Berni might have been a good lawyer, but he surely would have been a great diplomat.

Berni was no longer often seen around the city. When a friend reproached him for this, he answered, embarrassed, that his mother was ill and he had to visit her frequently in the Señora City. That was true. Doña Carmen had, for months, been showing degenerative symptoms of colon cancer. Berni no longer had the confident step he once had when the court called to request his services for a prisoner's defense. He wandered from one place to another without knowing where he walked.

One night, over drinks, his brother Arge told him it was just as well he hadn't graduated as a lawyer, because once practicing, he probably would have started tricking people who didn't know the law with word games. Hahaha—they both burst out laughing. Berni was being carried along by fate like a sheet of paper on the wind.

It looked like the end—but it was for Doña Carmen. Surrounded by family, friends from the Señora City of Buga, and people from Buenaventura and Cali, Doña Carmen died of esophageal cancer, which she had been suffering from for more than a year. At the funeral, her son Berni said: "Mother, you will not die forever, for you remain among us to keep company with your family. I—and we all—know that your spirit will stay to continue caring for us, blessing us, helping widows and anyone who needs you. You are an angel to us who have the joy of having you."

Berni spoke to his mother as if she were alive, but he couldn't go on. Others spoke and said that Doña Carmen had been mother number one among all mothers. Others said she had been the most self-sacrificing wife, who loved her "Monito," as she called him, above any known measure of love in the heart—a wife who honored every faithful, humble companion. People wept, just as Doña Carmen had—she lived half her life in tears. Eleven children; eleven history books with more moments of pain than happiness.

A woman who was not precisely Berni's wife came to transform him. Lilian, the secretary, slowly but surely drew Berni back to his obligations. She tended the office, reminded him of appointments, and, very tactfully, led him back to what he had abandoned: diligence in his work, attention to his family, his friends, and his clients.

She—Lilian—some years later would cause Berni a serious blood problem. Because of his hemophilia, even brushing his skin against hers caused a hematoma around the penile orbit. This would happen later in the United States, where she followed him—not as anything other than his secretary. She was in love.

In any case, Berni suffered inwardly, and one day he decided to leave everything and go to the northern country. He went with his whole family to the American Embassy in Bogotá and laid out their identification documents, passports, securities, title to their house, his car, and an excellent bank statement for his account. The package included visa applications for his wife, his three children, and himself.

The consul—using that psychology they're known for—stamped each passport without spending even a second reviewing the documents' validity.

The family returned the same day to the Sultana on the morning flight. Back home, with a glass of whiskey in hand—because he had to learn to drink "gringo urine," he joked—you could see him smile. After a sip, he said to his wife with mockery: "I've got to take aguardiente to the United States so those fools can learn to drink something good."

Berni was forced to send María Eugenia and the children ahead because the house sale and the rest of their belongings—the office and the car—couldn't be transacted as quickly as he had thought. He took his family to the airport and told them he would join them as soon as he sold his property. A year passed, then another, and Berni still hadn't been able to close any deal. But because he loved his wife and children so much, he visited them in Miami for Christmas—because, as in his parents' home, he would never miss the celebration of the birth of Jesus of Nazareth. After spending Christmas Eve and New Year's with them, he returned to Colombia but made a stop in Cartagena. There, he contacted managers of transport companies and, knowing truck drivers' need for cash after the banks closed so they could set out with their loads, he went back to the Sultana and sold—to the highest bidder but at a loss compared to going rates— everything he owned, house and car included.

Sixty days later, he was opening a storefront in Poblado del Bosque, within heroic Cartagena—the most beautiful city in the world for its architecture. Three cities in one: the old walled quarter protected by the Fort of San Fernando, built in colonial times; the modern city with its imposing towers, hotels and avenues, museums, and the lovely convention center set out over the waters of the Caribbean; and the other, medieval, with its vast residences of galleries, gardens, fountains, bridges, and a forest of tropical flora and fauna. Simply paradise. Its sea shows seven colors at noon every day. Cartagena is another jewel that sprang from the sea—more beautiful than San Juan, Havana, Miami, and others.

Berni went to visit representatives from banking, industry, and commerce. In less than a month, he was up to speed on the region's best businesses. In his new office, he cashed checks for truck owners, bought freight slips from transport companies, and advanced money on work contracts. This cycle returned him 1% of the principal—30% a month—so, after maintenance, representation, and taxes, he was on track to double his capital in under six months. In just five years, he would become one of the richest men in Colombia. He even sent his family in Miami $800 a month. On his trip to Miami last December, he left his wife, along with two cars paid in cash, $4,000, so they could move to New York, as his wife had told him it was easier to find work there for her and their sixteen-year-old daughter, who was getting ready to enroll at a university.

Berni worked twelve hours a day and made a lot of money, but nothing was perfect. In his lonely moments—despite being so sociable—he grew sad, immensely sad, when he remembered his children, whom he loved with all his heart and reason. Many times—dozens of times—he cried in sleepless nights over their separation. *I have to fix this*, he told himself more than once. *I'll bring them back to live in this city, and my life and theirs will be very different; close to me, they'll be safer as they grow, make progress, stay healthy, and reach their goals.* Once, in a formal conversation with one of the bank managers he visited daily, he asked, "What is happiness?" and Doctor Blanco answered, "Family." In truth, Berni had a lot of money, but he wasn't happy.

One night, in a bar, already past his limit on aguardiente and with a full glass in his hand, he said aloud, "I'll trade my life, I'll sell my life—either way I'm living it lost." Outside were the most beautiful women in Colombia and the November 11th carnival—and none of it interested him.

Berni could have gone to Miami at any time—he had a five-year visa—but his business required his personal presence, and it wasn't prudent to leave it with someone else. Besides, in the Heroic City, he had no acquaintance he could trust with such a promising future. In any case, he was thinking about his secretary, Lilian, who had stayed back in the Sultana and would surely follow him to be at his service—especially if she learned that Berni was suffering.

December came, and Berni prepared everything to travel. He bought clothes for his beloved and their children, along with gifts for his sister Luzmila, his brother Jaime, their children, and friends. He slipped $1,000 into his pocket and bought a bank check for $7,000, payable to himself in Miami. Then he went to the airport to board the plane to the Capital of the Sun. He knew the route, the city, the drill. It was his second trip to see his beloved wife and unforgettable children. It had been exactly a year since he'd seen María Eugenia, Carmen Eugenia, Bernardo, and Alberto, and his siblings. He also wanted to greet and hug everyone and tell them he wanted to bring his family back to Colombia—to the most beautiful city on the planet and its surroundings. He wanted to be completely happy and restore security to his loved ones, proving his love.

On the plane, he chatted with the passenger beside him, who asked if he spoke English. Berni answered that he spoke a little. "Anyway," he added, "we don't have to worry, because in Miami, the hard thing is finding someone who speaks English. There, the disobedient children of Fidel live—like modern Havana—Cubans everywhere and the odd North American." His companion smiled, relieved, and they kept talking.

Two hours and forty-five minutes after boarding, he was walking out through the international arrivals doors. He retrieved his luggage and headed outside to take a taxi. The driver was Latino, and Berni felt more at ease. They reached Miami Springs, but at the same address where Berni had stayed a year earlier, there was no one. The house was empty. Berni knocked at the neighbor's door, and no one answered; he did the same at the other side and got no reply either. "It's the hour—nobody's home," said the driver, who had already gotten out and, showing his watch, added that it was 3:30 in the afternoon. Berni went around back and, peering through a small window, could see the house was empty.

They got back in the taxi, and when the driver asked where to go next, Berni told him to take him to the address he showed him. He didn't find his brother there either; it was an address where Jaime had lived a year before. "How strange," Berni said, "nobody told me they'd moved, and they knew I was arriving today." It was

December 23. Berni—like his father—would never be without his family around him.

The taxi driver, apologizing, explained that in Miami, people leave a house easily to go somewhere else—some because they only have enough money to pay one month out of three, others to flee immigration, and the least because they buy their own home. "What's immigration?" Berni asked. "It's the Immigration agency—the one that chases the undocumented," he replied. "Ah, now I understand," said Berni. "All right, my friend, please take me to a hotel." Berni checked in and immediately made some calls. Then he asked the driver to stick with him for another two hours, because depending on a call, they might head back to the airport to buy a ticket. The man, who said his name was Jairo, agreed to stay if he was paid by the hour. "Of course, don't worry—I'll pay you by the hour," Berni said. After an hour, he used the phone and wrote down an address. He paid for the hotel and for the two lunches the driver ate—Berni didn't touch his—and they left for the airport. On the way, they talked, and Berni told him he'd been sending money to his family, to which the driver replied skeptically that it works the other way around—money is sent from here. "Sure, but my family doesn't have permission to work." "That doesn't matter," the driver said. "Undocumented people work—that's not a problem." As to how those without work permits could work, the man answered that it was very common to get a Social Security number or even a fake Social Security card. "What did you say, sir?" Berni exclaimed. "Getting a fake Social Security is a federal crime and is punished severely!" "That's true," said the driver, "but that's how it's done—and the government knows." Without realizing it, Berni was already getting out at the airport entrance. He paid again, handing the driver a $100 bill, and, saying goodbye, melted into the crowd waiting for their flights. He bought a ticket—so easily that it astonished him. The plane took off for New York. Berni was happy: in his pocket, he carried his wife's new address. He knew they would be moving there from Miami, but not when. "This must have happened just a few days ago—they didn't have time to let me know," he told himself. He leaned back and focused on the movie the flight attendant announced would be shown after the safety instructions. She also offered him the menu and, in passing, congratulated him on bringing a coat for the cold. "It's ten degrees in New York," she said. "New

York, New York," she said as she moved on, and Berni looked her up and down.

Berni couldn't have imagined, with all the imagination he possessed, what fate had in store for him. To stay awake, as he felt drowsy, he reached for his favorite book, *One Hundred Years of Solitude* by García Márquez, which he had been reading for the second time.

Without realizing it, he arrived at his destination. He tried to look out the window, but a heavy storm had obscured his view. He got out of the car, took a taxi, and handed the driver a written address. The taxi took him to the place where his wife and children were living—a place Berni, the most intelligent of Don Marco and Doña Carmen's sons, had come to. He stood at the door, having left everything behind for the moment to visit his beloved family and try to convince them to return to their adored homeland, where the El Dorado Berni had discovered in Cartagena de Indias—the port of the pirate Morgan—awaited them.

On that unforgettable night, at the end of the longest day of the century, Berni was almost too weak to take another step when he saw his wife, seven months pregnant. He had not seen her since December 31, exactly thirteen months earlier.

That night, Berni imagined himself in a thousand places, conversing with thousands of people, yet he couldn't align his plans. Exhausted, he begged God to cleanse his conscience, moving from rage to humility. Then, he cried out, "Thank you, Lord; tears are the balm of my soul."

A few minutes later, the light of dawn crept under the door. Before leaving for the airport, Berni asked about Herman—his wife's lover—and their son. His wife replied that she didn't know where to find him. Berni's son reproached him for not having sent any remittance in over six months, to which Berni replied, astonished, that he had never failed to send the money. "Do you see, guys?" his son Alberto said. "I suspected it. It's Herman who's taking the money for himself and telling us Dad has forgotten us."

111

On the plane ride to Miami, the capital of sunshine, Berni and his son talked about Hernán. Berni asked if his mother knew what Hernán did for a living. His son answered that his mother knew he was involved in drug trafficking. Berni then asked if Luzma, his aunt, was aware of Hernán's activities. Alberto replied, "Yes, Dad, my aunt knows everything. But she doesn't scold him because he provides her with everything she needs, and my aunt helps Mom since she's pregnant and wants to care for the grandchild. Aunt has been very kind to all of us since we've been living with her here in the United States."

Berni sighed, "What a shame this situation is. It hurts me that Hernán has fallen into drug trafficking. It's dangerous to be involved with those mafias. They forgive no one. He ought to know he'll end up either in prison or, God forbid, dumped on the side of the road with three or four bullets in his body."

Soon after, Berni's nephew Fernel returned to Miami, but due to a complication with his wife, his return to Cali had to be delayed. Lilian took care of Berni's new residence and his son Alberto, who was attending school and was a very well-rated, intelligent, quiet young man—and above all, a gentleman.

One day, Berni received a phone call. A man's voice told him, "Your nephew Hernán is in Baptist Hospital, in a coma; he could die at any moment." Berni asked for the caller's name, but he didn't identify himself and hung up without another word.

Half an hour later, Berni was in the emergency room at Baptist Hospital in Kendall. The place was unfamiliar to him. In the waiting area, besides his wife, were his sister—Hernán's mother—and other nieces and their friends. Berni hugged his sister and kissed her cheek. He shook his wife's hand and offered his condolences. At that very moment, he told her, from the bottom of his heart, that he was sorry for her loss. She burst into tears. Then Berni greeted everyone else and asked his sister to take him to see Hernán.

After passing through two rooms, they reached Hernán's bed. He was in a coma, alive only by the machines that kept him alive, but in reality, he was dead. His head had been destroyed by a point-blank

.45-caliber shot—an execution-style killing. The doctors told Berni that Hernán had been left in the hospital parking lot inside the vehicle he had rented in New Jersey. The police theory was that the perpetrators were likely relatives or friends of Hernán. "Yes, that theory makes sense, Doctor," said Berni.

Hernán's mother asked Berni for his opinion on whether they should disconnect Hernán from life support. Berni replied, "Sister, you are his mother, but it's not me you should ask—it's your son's wife." Unfortunately, Hernán's wife, Luzmila, hadn't come to the hospital. "It doesn't matter," Berni said. "Call her and consult her." "In my view, given your son's condition, he should be disconnected and left free—either to survive or to die."

Berni looked at his wife and refrained from asking her opinion. He thought, It should be the mother who decides.

After greeting a few others, Berni left the hospital, took the same car that had brought him there, and went home. There, he told his son and his secretary what had happened and stared at his son, who showed no reaction.

Before and after returning home, Berni received several calls, all of which he answered by expressing his condolences. He also stated that he didn't know why Hernán had been shot.

Lilian knew Berni needed to travel to the Heroic City to tend to his business but didn't know when. When she asked, Berni replied that he could go as soon as tomorrow. That's when Lilian told him that Fernel would be arriving again to propose a business deal. "Maybe so," Berni said, "but my pending business is more important."

Later that night, Lilian and Alberto went to bed. Berni kept watching TV. At 11 o'clock, they repeated the news of Hernán's murder. They announced that he had died.

The following day, officers arrived at Berni's house. At the police station, Berni realized they weren't city police officers, but agents of the Federal Bureau of Investigation (FBI). This made him nervous; he went pale, and his voice became halting. The agents noticed, but

Berni explained that his sister's grief over her son's death was overwhelming him. "Yes, it's lamentable," they said. "The victim was also your nephew, correct?" "Yes, Officer," he replied. Berni pulled himself together when he realized the agents were ordinary men with feelings. They began the usual round of questions: name, address, phone number, date of birth, profession, marital status, and, more pointedly, what he had been doing in Miami.

The agent asked, "Tell us when, how, and where you met Mr. Hernán Muñiz. When was the last time you saw him?"

Chapter 7
The Shadow of Sin

Berni answered in Spanish, as they offered him the option: "I've known Hernán since he was born in Cali, Colombia. He was my sister Luzmila's favorite son. The last time I saw him was last night at Baptist Hospital in this city, but before that, I hadn't seen him for two years and two months—since I visited Cali, and we met to talk about my wife and children, who had just moved to Miami."

"Where did Hernán live here in Miami?"

"He told me he lived with his wife, a daughter, and his mother—my sister Luzmila."

"Fine, continue."

"Then I went to live in Cartagena, and I didn't see him again."

"Did you know what he did for a living?"

"Well, he told me he brought a pickup truck down to sell and asked if I could name some possible buyers."

"What did you say?"

"I recommended two possible buyers."

"Who were they?"

"I don't remember their names."

"If he had a sewing workshop, why did he take a truck to sell in Cali?"

"I don't know."

"Was your wife, María Eugenia, his lover, friend, or girlfriend?"

"Friend."

"Do you know if they ever had a relationship beyond friendship?"

"I don't know."

"The man you saw in the hospital last night—was that Hernán Muñiz?"

"Yes, Officer."

"When was the last time you saw your wife, Señora María Eugenia Gómez?"

"Last night at the hospital."

"Was she alone?"

"No, she was with my sister, the victim's mother."

"Did Hernán have enemies?"

"I don't know."

"Do you suspect anyone who might have shot him?"

"No, Officer."

"Can you describe his character?"

"Somewhat hot-tempered—he easily got into arguments or fights."

"Did he use drugs?"

"No."

"Did he drink?"

"Yes."

"Did he smoke?"

"No."

"Do you know his siblings?"

"Yes."

"How many?"

"Four."

"Does his father live?"

"Yes."

"We're going to take your photograph; it's routine."

After the photo, the agent said, "Mr. Berni, we need you to remain in the city. Please provide any information that could help clarify the investigation. We know you have business in Cartagena, but you cannot leave the city until we inform you otherwise. Thank you for your cooperation. You'll hear from us soon. Take my card and keep it."

"Thank you, Officer. Please take my card as well, and call me whenever you think it's appropriate," Berni said, though he only offered it out of courtesy. "Thanks."

Berni left quickly, hailing the first taxi outside. "Take me home," he instructed. It was four in the afternoon.

That night at the hospital, Berni saw his beloved María Eugenia face-to-face. She was as beautiful as ever, though more confused than ever.

The day after his hospital visit, the FBI agents came asking for Berni, son of Don Marco and Doña Carmen. Berni learned this at Miami's central police station. He had visited many police stations in his home country, but this was the first time he'd been taken to one as a suspect in a crime—a murder. A felony, as they call homicide or serious crime in the United States.

When Berni returned home, the house was full of relatives and friends. As always, he remained cordial with everyone despite the long day. Questions came from all directions, and he answered them without committing himself. When one bolder guest asked if he could leave the country, Berni replied, "Yes."

"Strange," the man replied. "In these cases, they don't let a person leave the city, much less the country. In special circumstances, they even take the suspect's passport."

Berni remained quiet, but privately acknowledged to himself that this was true.

They had coffee, and when someone suggested a toast with aguardiente, Lilian, the secretary, spoke up to say there was none. Later, at the first opportunity, she pulled Berni aside and explained that there was liquor, but she didn't recommend drinking in such a situation. Berni knew her well and didn't argue with her. Lilian wasn't like most Colombians who drank aguardiente because the sun came out—and if by chance it didn't, they drank because it hadn't.

At the gathering, Berni learned that Hernán's body would be taken to New Jersey for a Christian burial at a Catholic cemetery in Union City.

The next day, Lilian asked if she should unpack the suitcases. Berni told her to leave them ready. "I want us to go to the stores now and buy clothes," Lilian said, and Berni agreed.

That night, Berni made a series of calls—first to his children, Berni Jr. and Carmen Eugenia. He spoke to his sister Luzmila and offered any help she might need. He did the same with María Eugenia, his wife. He called others as well. In Cali, he left a message for his nephew Fernel. Close to midnight, Fernel returned the call and promised to come back to Miami within a week or two at most.

Berni also called Cartagena and informed a colleague that he would be delayed another week because of a last-minute issue. The colleague said the business was going well and there had been no problems.

Two weeks passed, and things were worsening for Berni. He kept in touch with most of the people he had contacted, but the answers were discouraging. His nephew Fernel still couldn't travel. His family in Union City refused any financial help, and his two children—who had promised to move to Miami and then to Cartagena—now didn't want to leave their mother alone. When Berni insisted, they told him that they loved their mother dearly and wouldn't abandon her in such a difficult time. Berni accepted this, but internally thought, *Damn it—will this wretch keep causing me trouble even after he's dead?*

When Berni realized the situation, there was nothing he could do. His hands were tied.

Upon returning home, Berni was met with the news that Fernel couldn't arrive for at least three more months—he had been detained in Cali over a bad check issue, and to make matters worse, a fraud complaint had been added. This forced Berni to change all his plans—his own future, his children's future, and Lilian's future. Though she had nothing to do with the funeral, she ended up "burned by the candle wax." She suffered with Berni—perhaps more than Berni himself—because she had grown fond of his children, especially Alberto, who lived with her and whom she helped with his homework, just as his own mother would have done. Alberto, though quiet and saying nothing, understood the problems his mother was facing in New Jersey. He was young enough to want to play, but he didn't. He didn't want to play. He was the youngest of Berni's children and had suffered the most from the situation.

Berni called Cartagena and asked his manager to send all the capital using the power of attorney Berni had left him. The manager confirmed he would. When Berni asked what to say to the bank and transport company managers and business contacts, the manager was told to say nothing and to obtain capital to keep the business going.

"This assignment of my commercial rights—you don't have to pay me for it; that's how the document I'm sending will read."

Berni waited for the money—already converted into dollars—but instead, it turned into a lawsuit from a lawyer friend practicing in Cartagena. Berni never heard another word about the partner, the money, or the assignment document or contract.

"It looks," a police officer remarked years later when Berni returned, "as if the sea swallowed them."

"Could it be the Bermuda Triangle, Officer?" Berni asked.

"Yes, yes—possibly," the officer replied.

On the flight back, Berni thought his country would sink into the sea—a sea of crime, common crooks, and those in suits. It was the summer of 1987. As a premonition, his country would sink thirteen years later.

Berni found himself forced to trade money for happiness. He bought happiness: he was content with his children by his side. He had to accept the loss of the capital he had left in his country. He decided to start looking for a job. Meanwhile, his nephew Fernel didn't reappear. He, too, had serious problems in Cali—the same kind Berni had: financial and romantic. They were two people with much in common, but Fernel's greed for money led him to a federal prison in the United States for ten years, for narcotics trafficking.

Berni went out every day searching for work, but since he didn't speak English, he couldn't land a skilled job. He sent out résumés, but at interviews, the "diplomats," as he called them, told him they'd call as soon as a position opened. He understood—and since he didn't know any manual trade like A/C technician, nursing, mechanics, or carpentry—he began looking toward New York. It was the capital of the world, and there was a world of work there.

He had Alberto with him, but his other children—Berni Jr. and Carmen Eugenia—wouldn't be joining him.

"Yes. That was settled in the last conversation."

As always, Lilian came to Berni's rescue once again. She called her cousin, whom she loved like a sister, and the cousin invited her—and anyone else who wished—to live at her home in New York. She also said she could help Lilian get a job at a jewelry shop doing work she hadn't yet learned, and she could line up a job for Berni as a car driver in a parking garage—a "jockey," as they call it in the city that never sleeps. In Miami, they were called valet parking attendants.

Lilian and Alberto left, but Alberto returned to his mother's home. Berni was separated from his son, but they would be living only forty miles apart. A week later, Berni arrived in New York, and the very next day he was employed by a parking management company in Manhattan. At first, he didn't drive, but two months later, he was handling cars coming in and out.

Berni spoke with the FBI agent in charge of the Miami investigation, and he was granted permission to relocate to New York after registering the new address. He asked for his travel document back, but the agent didn't return it. He was also told the investigation hadn't advanced—"because in cases like this—drug trafficking—you don't get witnesses or testimony."

Another month passed, and Berni still hadn't been switched to a day shift by the operations director. His hours were 10 p.m. to 6 a.m. Berni went to the office, left the garage keys on the desk, offered his thanks, and prepared to go home. His boss, Francisco, asked why he was quitting. Berni replied that he'd been promised a day shift.

"Yes, of course. Give me a few more days; I promise I'll move you," Francisco said.

"All right," Berni replied. "I'll wait the days you want—but at home. On this shift, you can't sleep, and the only people who don't need to sleep at night are prostitutes."

Francisco gave him a new schedule, and starting the next day, Berni began working at another location, where he stayed for more than three years.

121

Every Sunday, Berni would buy a bus ticket, happily take his seat, and ride to his children's house. He would pick up small gifts or birthday presents in the shops. Lilian went shopping with her cousin.

After an hour's ride from New York to Union City, Berni arrived at their door. He rang the bell once, twice, three times. He waited—maybe they were in the bathroom and couldn't hear. He rang again—nothing. He waited another half hour. Maybe, he told himself, they couldn't hear over the loud music. He rang four, five, six times. "Fine, I'll come back next Sunday," he said.

The next Sunday was the same. Other Sundays, he thought, *Maybe they're back from vacation. Great, I'll hug and kiss them and not mention the wasted trips. Why say it, if it won't happen again?* No one was home. He searched for a note that might have blown down, but found nothing. He headed back and, at Times Square station, got lost in the underground maze leading to different lines. He was so depressed that life felt small. He couldn't find the exit or the entrance to the 7 train that would take him to 48th Street on Roosevelt Avenue in Queens, where the Colombian community lived. He had rehearsed telling his children how much he loved them—but they didn't care. He phoned them after three hours had passed, but no answer.

He wandered out to the street aimlessly, not caring which street it was. He walked, thought, and walked, crying as he went. He cried and cried, walked and no longer thought, then sat on the first bench he found. Unaware, he had ended up in Central Park. He cried for three, then five hours—time, day, life didn't matter. He cried more in those few hours than he had when his father drowned in the Cauca River in Colombia.

He wept for his children, then for his parents. He remembered he had been a bad son. *That's it—now I see clearly. I sowed nothing, and now I can reap nothing. I have to end this.*

Just then, the No. 4 train rumbled by beneath where he sat, heading for the Bronx. He thought how easy it would be to jump—just down a few stairs, toss his papers into the storm drain, his body onto the rails, and it would all be over. He looked up, as if searching for God, but then a sound distracted him. In the basket where he'd left a gift and a cake, he saw a squirrel and some birds eating what she dropped. A dove lifted off and slipped into the branches of a tree. Berni followed the dove carefully and discovered a nest with three chicks.

Enraptured, he heard a woman's voice, "Good afternoon, mister. Very nice day today," as she walked past.

Berni walked a few steps, called home, and asked for Lilian. He told her where he was, what he was seeing, and invited her to come see the park. She agreed at once, and an hour later, they were strolling and admiring the beauty of the place. They lunched at a nearby restaurant and then took a train to Brooklyn. Berni and Lilian stood rapt in front of the Botanic Garden. Berni thought again and accepted that his children should—and could—make their own lives, their own stories. *"They are my children, but they're not mine."*

"I have to move forward—each of us seeks our destiny, and I must accept mine. They don't have to wait for me. Lilian doesn't have to wait for me." He told her as they admired the garden's flowers.

Berni's world receded. *I have to forget my past. My town—now a new sun will light me. I won't relive my sexual adventures, my university days. I'll never again stand by the riverbank watching my father's drowned body drift by.*

Distracted, Berni heard Lilian call out: "Look over there—a black flower. A black rose." They were both amazed and understood why the Little Prince had fallen in love with a rose. She drew close and reminded him that Colombia has the most beautiful roses in the world.

"Yes, that's true," Berni said. He plucked a red rose from the nearest bush and gave it to Lilian. She hugged him, gazing into his eyes, and Berni slowly brought his lips to hers. In that kiss, Lilian felt herself unfurl, and Berni felt like a bee sipping honey. In that moment, Berni began a new life.

"Truly," Lilian said, "life must be lived—but we have to learn how to live it, and whoever does, reaches happiness." Berni replied, "Some learn early, and others late, but it's always worth it."

The next day, Lilian phoned Berni at the factory—where he worked the 7 a.m. to 3 p.m. shift—and told him to stop by and greet her friend, his nephew's ex-wife, before heading to his second job at the garage from 4 p.m. to midnight, when it closed. He did stop by and found María de las Mercedes, a beautiful woman in her well-kept forties. She had already separated from a son of Berni's eldest brother. He had met her in Miami before moving to New York. They greeted each other, and Berni promised to come back early to take her out to eat. "I'll stop by my boss's and ask him to send someone to cover me. I'll be back at 7 p.m."

Berni, María, and Lilian went in search of a good seafood restaurant—María's favorite. During dinner, when María learned that Berni didn't have legal status in the country, she proposed marriage. For Berni, it was a great surprise—and even more so for Lilian, who excused herself and went to the bar. A door had opened for Berni to obtain U.S. residency because María had been a permanent resident for years. Lilian didn't return immediately, and María used the opportunity to tell him she wasn't doing it for money, but because "I have always loved you." Berni was even more confused, but fortunately, Lilian returned just then. She had been crying, though she tried to hide it. Berni noticed.

In any case, Lilian's return helped—Berni didn't know how to answer María.

"Tomorrow, I have to go back to Los Angeles, but I'll return in two weeks—on November 9th. Have everything ready for us to go get married." María spoke with certainty—the wedding would be in two months.

Afterward, they went to listen to old-time music and reminisced about their days in Cali when María had lived with César Jr., the son of Berni's brother Julio César—the most "couple-like" couple who ever lived.

Berni accepted and thanked María for her noble gesture. Raising a glass of aguardiente—something he was very good at—he invited them to toast. Linking his arm with María's, he kissed her cheek. "Long live María, long live life, long live Lilian," he said loudly, standing up. That night, each slept in their own bed, and Berni fell sound asleep, while the women talked past midnight. Lilian thought that, in some way, time would favor her, because Berni could give her residency after separating from María. But when would that be? Or would she lose him forever?

María knew Lilian was Berni's secretary, but not that she was in love with him. Lilian didn't tell her that night, fearing María might back out of marrying Berni.

The next day, Berni went to the attorney his boss recommended and paid 50% of the costs to obtain a divorce from María Eugenia—the woman he had loved so much, who had given him three children he loved immensely, and whom, at this point in his life, he didn't even know if he could forget. Two months later, Berni received the court's divorce decree and married María de las Mercedes in a solemn—though civil—ceremony.

That night, in the hotel room, María fell asleep while Berni took his "wedding bath." The price of that was that the brand-new husband filtered his honey through the body of a woman who had been waiting for him—had been waiting twelve years, eleven months, ten days, and nine hours—since the day she first saw him at the Panamanian consulate in Cali, where she was secretary to the "widow with dignity" who owned an insurance agency Berni advised. She had been counting the days. She confessed that night to the one man she had loved and would love forever. That woman was Lilian, who had taken the room next to the newlyweds'.

Berni got up—or pretended to—from the sofa in María's room and, excusing himself, went out to get a newspaper. On the front page of *The New York Times* was an announcement of a general amnesty for all foreigners without legal status—the undocumented.

María did not demand any payment from her husband. She made that clear. Nonetheless, Lilian did something double-edged: the next day, visiting María in her hotel room, she gifted her a round-trip ticket to Colombia—specifically to Cali. The date was open. "Use it any day you like—today, tomorrow, whenever." On the other hand, it could, at any time, serve as a kind of "payment." Lilian had heard María say she hadn't visited her country in three years. María received it joyfully, hugged Lilian, and whispered, "God repay you." A week later, the plane carrying her took off from LaGuardia Airport in New York, bound for Cali.

Berni got back to the hotel at 4:45 and went straight to bed. There was Lilian, on the very side where Berni had seen María for a solid week. Before losing himself in his secretary's kisses, he whispered in her ear: "You'll be the happiest woman in the universe, because only with you will this honeymoon last a lifetime."

No one at all knew where Berni and Lilian were—indeed, not even they knew. For three days, they stayed in the same hotel, in the same bed, without even knowing whether María had arrived in Cali.

Berni was temporarily put in charge of company advertising. His task was to bring in new garage clients. The team consisted of six men, including Berni as supervisor. One of them was a young man from Esmeraldas, Ecuador. He seemed wholesome—and he was—but also very naïve. One morning, he showed Berni a letter to send to Ecuador and asked how to mail it. Berni took him to the corner mailbox and told him to drop the envelope in. Before doing it, the young man asked how the postal employees would know his letter was for Esmeraldas, Ecuador, if they only spoke English.

"You're right," Berni said, and then told him that when he lifted the mailbox flap, he should shout, "Mister, my letter is going to Ecuador!" The young man yelled so loudly he had a cough from then on. It went away a year later, after he spoke—in English—to the clerk at the post office.

Meanwhile, Berni received an appointment to appear with his wife at Immigration at the U.S. embassy in Colombia. He took the letter to the police officer, who returned his passport because his case had already been transferred to New York some time earlier. He flew to Bogotá alone, even though family and friends told him he should take his wife. María recommended he take the risk, since she couldn't travel—she had a new job she couldn't afford to lose. Berni agreed and saw the logic; in a way, it helped him, because he hadn't slept in two nights thinking that he and his wife alone in Bogotá—with those cold, romantic nights—he wouldn't be able to stay faithful to Lilian.

Berni boarded the plane for his destiny—alone, without her, without Lilian, whom he invited at the last minute. She couldn't travel—or rather, she could leave the country, but she had no way back; she was undocumented. To Berni's surprise, she said, "Don't you want to meet your new child—our child?"

"What do you mean?" Berni replied.

And she, hugging and kissing his lips, said softly, "I'm going to be the mother of your child. Even if I could travel, I shouldn't fly. I'm pregnant."

She wouldn't do it because the first three months of pregnancy are essential for the fetus's development. She spoke as if she had experience, though this was her first child, her first man, her first love.

Berni was receiving the best gift a man could receive: a child. The news injected new vigor into him. You could see his happiness; his stride became quick and determined again. His mind was clear. He knew this child was a blessing from God because, with humility, he had accepted losing his children—the beloved offspring from his marriage with María Eugenia. During this time, he also learned they were packing their suitcases to return to live in Miami.

On the flight to Bogotá, Berni chatted with the other passengers. He met a Colombian man who lived in White Plains, near New York, and who also had an appointment at the embassy the day after Berni. Without leaving his seat, Berni bought a new car from him without even seeing it. He paid for it right there, and the seller handed him a note for a woman named Esperanza, who would deliver the car to him upon his return. The man introduced himself as Gustavo Williams and said he was born in Armenia, Colombia.

Berni arrived at the embassy. An hour later, they called him in. The officer invited him to sit and asked about his wife. Berni glanced back and, without showing his face, replied, "She stayed outside, talking with a friend she ran into in the garden."

"Fine, no problem," the officer said. "Sign here," he pointed to a spot on the paper, and then handed Berni a large envelope, explaining it could only be opened by the immigration officer at the airport in Miami. The whole procedure took only five minutes, and Berni hurried out. He left the embassy without saying goodbye to the others waiting there—people who would only ask questions that made those waiting even more nervous.

At the embassy door, he took a taxi to the hotel. "Please wait for me," he said confidently, "ten minutes. Then, if you can, take me to the airport." The driver waited—exactly the kind of fare every cabbie hopes for. True to his word, Berni came back, and the car sped off toward the airport. The taxi driver, impressed, commented that people who had lived in the United States learned to do things quickly and precisely.

"Yes, that's true, sir," Berni replied, smiling at him through the rearview mirror.

Berni flew to Cali. The visa allowed him to stay in Colombia for 30 days—the envelope had to be delivered in Miami within that period. However, Berni wouldn't stay longer than ten days—just enough to enjoy them to the fullest. The day after his arrival, he was seen on the streets of Juanchito, a woman on one arm and a bottle of aguardiente in the other. He visited all the dance halls, eventually ending up at "Agapito," telling his companion, "This place brings back many fond memories." When dawn broke, they went to the bank of the Cauca River and sat down. Berni convinced the young woman that at six in the morning, a man's body would float by, and he always waited there to say goodbye. She agreed to wait with him. When Berni, crying and shouting, told her it was floating by, she covered her eyes. Berni stood and moved closer to the water, as if he wanted to jump in, but the woman grabbed his jacket and pulled him to the ground. "Do you see him? Look—there he goes. That's my father; he passes by here every day." They stayed there for two hours. When they "woke up," Berni drank a double shot to steady himself.

"Where are we going?" his companion asked.

"I'm going to take you to another place where you'll see the stars again, but closer—much, much closer. And instead of fear, you'll feel something very special." The hotel room's ceiling had a beautiful painting of the firmament.

At the airport, Berni presented his passport, ticket, and police record to the DAS (Administrative Department of Security) agent. The officer checked the wanted list and found Berni's name with both surnames—paternal and maternal.

"You can't travel, sir—you're on this list of fugitives," the officer said, calling on the radio-telephone.

Berni thought for a moment and then said, "My certificate, which you have in your hands, attests that I am in good standing with this country's laws. It's dated just eight days ago, in downtown Bogotá. Your wanted list is a year and two months old. So, my honorable officer, you'd be making a mistake by not letting me leave the country."

"Your certificate could be fake," the officer remarked, just as two more police officers arrived in response to his call.

"If you insist on that, I can stay as long as necessary to prove otherwise—and incidentally earn a fabulous sum from the government at your expense, from a lawsuit," Berni said. (His tone made the officer change his attitude.)

"I wouldn't go so far as to say it's fake," the officer replied, "but it is suspicious that it was issued."

"Look, sir," said Berni, "I have an order from the Sole Criminal Court of the Circuit of Tunja, dated ten days ago—earlier than the certificate—where the Honorable Judge records that the complaint

129

is against a namesake, not me. The thing is, I didn't think it necessary to bring it with me, so it's already on board."

"That's not a problem," said the conscientious officer. "I can have it brought here right now."

"Proceed at once then, because I could miss my flight," Berni insisted.

Chapter 8
New Lands: Union City

At that moment, a major commotion broke out. Personnel from the police, DAS, FBI, DEA, airline employees, and the press were in motion. The plane, already on the runway, was ordered to halt its takeoff. The crew was instructed to retrieve Berni's suitcase, marked with the name "Berni Gómez." It took an hour, and the airport came to a standstill. Only officials, airline employees, and journalists moved about. Hundreds of people gathered at the balconies, eyes fixed on the jet bound for Miami. For every Colombian traveling abroad, on average, six people came to see them off, and with a full flight, there were 1,800 people at the airport.

One woman told another that the man must have two kilos of cocaine in his suitcase. Another said it was probably a swindler, and the suitcase was full of jewelry. A man loudly declared he was ready to scoop up the bills that would fly down the runway. An old man told another that it was either weapons—or a bomb. Everyone had a theory, but no one thought it might be judicial evidence.

The suitcase was tossed onto the tarmac. Surrounded by more than fifteen people, Berni opened it and took out the document. He immediately handed it to the senior DAS officer. The plane resumed its journey, and Berni went back to the offices to wait for the airline to issue him a new ticket.

Berni boarded his flight at 11 a.m.—seven hours after his original departure.

Upon arriving in New York, Berni had no residency and no envelope. The immigration officer in Miami told him the envelope would be mailed to his address, but his passport was stamped.

It was seven in the morning when Berni started work—three days earlier than the vacation days he had left. The owner of the company—an honorable and respected Jewish man—knew him, and

131

his immediate boss, a Colombian gentleman who spoke perfect English, liked Berni so much that other employees asked if the boss was his son.

"His name is Francisco Gómez, but I'm not his father," Berni Gómez—son of Doña Carmen and Don Marco, both deceased—would reply.

The company leased most of the parking garages in Manhattan. On the day they opened a new location, all the supervisors were there, including Francisco, the owner, and ten attendants to park the cars—Berni among them. The owner, Mr. Zuiss, was in the office near Berni and the bathroom—the most important place in New York, especially Manhattan. Mr. Zuiss pointed to the bathroom and asked, "Is it in use?"

"No, sir," Berni replied.

The man stood there waiting but couldn't hold it and wet his pants. Berni couldn't stop laughing and called Francisco over to ask why Mr. Zuiss hadn't used the bathroom. That moment caused a commotion—an emergency meeting was called, and the garage doors were closed. After an hour of discussion, interpreting English and Spanish semantics, they reopened, but Francisco called Berni into his office and ordered him to go work at another site. He advised Berni to study English. The next day, a memo circulated stating that any employee who didn't speak English had to speak with management. Job applicants now had to be bilingual. Berni was reassigned to a lot in Queens, where the customers spoke Spanish. A month later, Berni handed in his resignation, explaining to his boss that Latin Americans hadn't learned to tip, and his income had dropped significantly, upsetting his budget.

The next day, Berni was working at Rapid Park. He recovered financially and began shopping with Lilian, as their child was already moving and almost talking. It was a boy, as shown on the sonogram, where "he could be clearly seen."

"It was Halloween, October 31st—the witches were out on the street. The warlocks, too. Berni never scared anyone, but he loved

132

being scared, so he went to a party looking for a fright. When he got home, his wife was waiting to tell him she was in labor. He almost died of fright. Since her water hadn't broken, Berni suggested they wait, but he started timing the contractions. He knew that if the pains came every ten minutes, it was time to go to the hospital.

At daybreak, Berni suggested they go out walking so she would dilate. "You know," he told her, "doctors prefer to do a C-section to avoid risks, and neither you nor I want that, right?"

"Right," Lilian replied, and they walked down the five flights of stairs, reached the street, and walked about ten blocks. Berni talked the whole time to distract her, supporting her by the shoulders. Suddenly, a car pulled over—it was his niece and her husband. They offered help, and Lilian asked Berni to accept.

They reached the hospital and entered through the emergency room. Once there, Lilian's water broke, and the pains came every ten minutes. At three in the afternoon, Berni's son cried for the first time. Lilian was already crying from emotion, fear, and happiness. Berni cried with happiness, just as he had when the children María Eugenia gave him were born.

"He's a clone," said the doctor. "You can already see he's identical to his father."

In New York, the capital of the world, a human being had been cloned—many years before science suspected it could be done. He had everything his father had. He wasn't just similar—he was exactly the same. Thirteen years later, Marco Antonio—as the priest who baptized him named him—would acknowledge he also had his father's mind. He was the top student in eighth grade, just as his father had been in primary school, secondary school, and at university.

After Marco Antonio's birth, his mother looked very happy and smiled easily—something she had never done before. Family began to come to the apartment to see the beautiful baby; neighbors and friends arrived. Berni's children—who hadn't used to visit him— came to see their brother constantly. They learned to love him.

133

Berni devoted himself to his son. He was no longer seen out on the street or at parties with friends, who teased him, saying Lilian had become his handbrake.

History repeated itself with Marco Antonio, just as it had forty years earlier with Berni, the son of Doña Carmen and Don Marco, back in the Miracle City: people formed a procession to meet the beautiful child born at Christmas and lent to the Sisters of Saint Vincent de Paul to be placed in the Nativity scene.

Berni was working, badly distracted, in the car-lot garage when he noticed a man watching him, not missing a single move. It was a dark autumn afternoon, the temperature around 6 degrees Fahrenheit. The man wore an overcoat, hat, and gloves. Berni went over and, when he asked if he could help him, realized it was his nephew Fernel, Argemiro's son. The last time they'd spoken by phone in Miami, two years earlier, Fernel had told Berni he'd be back in two weeks. It took him two years. Berni loved him so much that he hugged him and said, "Thank God you're alive."

"Why do you say that, Berni?"

"Well, I didn't hear anything from you, and on top of that, your father called asking me if I'd seen you or knew where you might be."

"Berni," Fernel shot back, "you're an idiot. I've been watching you for a while, working like an ant. Look how skinny you've gotten, busting your back for these gringos at eight dollars an hour. Don't be a fool—come with me and stop giving your life away to these exploiters, these gringo sons of bitches" (he never said "hijueputas," only "hijuepuchas").

"Give me a few minutes," Berni answered, and went to ask his immediate supervisor for the rest of the afternoon off. On the way home, he bought a bottle of aguardiente to share with his nephew— whom he loved like a brother.

An hour later, they walked into Berni's place. Lilian greeted them, surprised—it was 5 p.m., and Berni usually got home at 9. They sat down, and Lilian offered them food.

After dinner, Lilian set the bottle on the table, and they toasted to a new life, to the children, to Fernel's parents, to the wives—"TO THEM," Berni said softly so Lilian wouldn't hear; she had ears like the walls and was in the kitchen washing the dishes. Fernel sprawled out, and between insults toward Americans and praise for Berni, said he had excellent connections in Los Angeles and San Francisco. "I want you to come with me, work little, and make a lot of money. I can't stand seeing you work in this weather for peanuts"—Berni checked in and returned an average of 200 cars a day.

"This job," Berni said, "is hard—especially for people like me, at forty-seven."

"Bernito, I love you," Fernel said. "So get everything in order and let's go. I need you because you're someone I can trust, and the job I'm offering is pure trust."

Berni sat thinking and remembered he'd been offered something similar in Miami. "Yeah," he thought, "same line of business." Like his father, after a few shots of aguardiente, Berni tended to speak more plainly, and he asked, "Chubs, that job I'd be doing over there—does it have anything to do with drugs?"

"Well, not exactly," his nephew answered. "Basically you'll be in an elegant, furnished house in a residential area and you'll spend the whole day watching TV."

"Nothing else?" Berni asked.

"On weekends, I'll come by with one or two cars, one or two guys, and they'll leave you the keys. Then, two or three hours later, someone you'll identify with a passphrase will pick up the keys and take the cars, one or two, whichever. So you'll only ever handle keys, nothing else."

"Chubs, I've already introduced you to my son with Lilian—he's only eight months old—and when he was born, I promised I'd care for him, educate him, and see him through university. I don't want what happened with the kids María gave me to happen again—

135

through my irresponsibility, I haven't gotten them through college, and I don't think I'll be able to now."

"I don't think it's your fault," Fernel said. "What happened is destiny changed the plans you had for them—and Hernán was part of that destiny."

"No, Chubs, I don't want to, and shouldn't, blame anyone for my family breaking up!"

"Don't be dumb—the whole thing is Hernán's fault, and your woman's, or rather María Eugenia's. Or are you scared?"

"The truth is, now I am afraid—afraid something unexpected will happen and I won't see my kids or Lilian again," Berni said—to avoid sounding like a doom-sayer by naming the fall and, as a result, prison.

"But Berni, I'm telling you—there's no danger. I'll even take Lilian and your son Marco, or, if you want, all four of you!"

"No, Chubs, they're not coming with me."

"Berni, forgive me, but I don't recognize you—you're not the Berni I visited in Miami."

"Well," Berni replied, "times change. I remember," he added, "going to that address in Coconut Grove to pick up the famous 'doll'—what the narco mafia calls each kilo of cocaine, wrapped in cloth and then plastic—and when I came back home escorted by a squad car with two cops, do you remember the diarrhea that gave you? Chubs? And you call me a coward?"

"Oh, I remember perfectly, Bernito. But don't tell me you weren't also scared—scared in your pants, yes or no?"

"I won't deny I was scared, but in my pants? No."

"Whereas you had diarrhea for more than three days."

"Well, that's because the beating I gave my wife kept it going," he shot back.

Here's what happened: Berni went to pick up a "doll" at the place Chubs sent him, to test whether he had the guts to join the organization. Very cleverly, Berni figured the best way to avoid the police stopping him and finding the merchandise—a kilo of cocaine—was to have them escort him home. Without realizing it, Berni was inaugurating a new era in U.S. drug trafficking, because from then on the drugs would be escorted, in most cases, by police cruisers. That's how it went: a man Berni didn't know—and would never see again—left a package with the "doll" in his car's trunk, closed it, and, as if nothing, Berni flagged down a passing squad car. He told the officer in Spanish that he needed help; when the driver didn't understand, Berni called over a bystander and asked him to tell the officers in English to lead him to the address he showed them— he said he was a tourist and couldn't find it. The officers told the volunteer to tell Berni to follow them. Fifteen minutes later Berni was arriving at his house, escorted by a Miami police cruiser. At that moment, his nephew Fernel, watching from the living-room window, bolted for the bathroom. The diarrhea lasted three days.

"And where the hell did you take the 'doll'?"

"Oh, Bernito, we ate it—it was a frozen chicken from the supermarket. I brought it back, and your secretary cooked it."

Both burst out laughing, looked at each other, and kept laughing.

Between one shot and the next, Fernel kept urging Berni to pack his bags. Berni responded that he wouldn't abandon his family. "Don't waste your time, Chubs. Look—better go back to Colombia and be with your father; he needs you, and at his side, you can become a very rich man. Transport is one of the best businesses in the world, and you know that's true. Your old man's company," Berni said emphatically, trying to persuade him, "has a great reputation, and under my brother's wing, you'll grow it. Besides, Arge already wants to begin transitioning management to someone else; he told me so recently—he even asked me to run it."

(Chubs started lowering his head and stopped pressing Berni.) "And a few days ago, I read in *The New York Times* that the government is going to allocate $10 billion to fight drugs. They'll recruit thousands of undercover agents—drivers, hotel cooks, public-school teachers—the war will be total. Plus, they're introducing a bill to double the prison terms for conspiracy, distribution, sale, and use of narcotics. How about that, dear Chubs?" Berni finished.

"Look, Bernito, you don't know these gringo sons of bitches. Everything they do or say is exaggerated. But when the moment comes, they go halfway or less. They can't—and don't want to—end drugs because they're the best customers for buying and using them. Remember what I'm telling you now, at the end of 1986: they fight it only for show. The moment will come when they themselves legalize it. Colombia, Ecuador, Bolivia, Peru, and Mexico together couldn't legalize it—but the United States will, when it wants to."

"Fine," Berni said. "Nothing you're saying is crazy. But don't forget—until that happens, I, you, or anyone in the business could spend years in the shadows, in jail or prison, depending on the charges the prosecutor brings."

"Your parents love you and are waiting," he added. "Let me dial your dad so you can tell him you love him!" (In Colombian families, once a bottle of aguardiente is gone, feelings pour out, and everyone, one by one, grabs the phone to call relatives.) While Berni dialed, Chubs had already started crying, and Berni hurried to place the call because the poor guy was sobbing inconsolably—and worst of all, he cried horribly; his mouth looked like a deflated car tire.

Lilian kept telling Berni that living like this was better than living in a cell. "There's no valid excuse for those who seek easy money at the cost of their life or freedom."

"You're right," Berni said.

The next day, Berni picked up the family car he had bought from a fellow passenger on his Bogotá trip to get his U.S. residency. Clearly, Berni—and Lilian—had no calling to be drug-trafficking mules.

Three months after Fernel had stayed at Berni's house—and after Berni warned him about the anti-drug measures, and precisely six months after the first warning—Fernel fell into the hands of the DEA in Los Angeles, together with a former driver from the company in Buenaventura, Colombia.

At Christmas, Colombians customarily gather as families to celebrate the Nativity. Gifts are exchanged, and people also make promises to parents, siblings, or friends—to finish school, change jobs, or finally complete something left undone. Fernel knelt before his father—whom he loved more than one loves a simple-minded son—and promised never again to traffic drugs. "Father, to keep this promise, I won't return to the United States. I'll dedicate myself to your transport company here in Buenaventura." His father, Argemiro, who loved him more than one loves a "foolish" son, hugged him, raised the aguardiente, and invited him to toast to his word as a man. They forgave each other and cried for a long time until they fell asleep on the living-room sofa.

Not a month had passed when Fernel, telling his father he was going to Cali to buy clothes, went straight to Palmaseca's Bonilla Aragón airport and bought a ticket to Los Angeles, California.

The phone rang at Berni's place up in New York. "Hello, who's this?" he said...

Fernel bowed his head like the Japanese—but not out of obedience or respect, rather from drunkenness.

The next day, he left Berni's house looking for a driver who lived in Queens, New York. An hour later, the two of them were on a flight to Los Angeles.

Berni and Lilian were living in an apartment on the 5th floor of a building with more than 40 units, subsidized by the local government, where they paid only $390 a month in rent. They had to go up and down the stairs every day to get to work. They took their son to the care of a very kind, loving family—Marco Antonio, Lilian's firstborn and Berni's fourth child, only a few months old. The woman who looked after Berni's son was very beautiful, elegant, and refined, notably educated and cultured, originally from Peru, a country south of Colombia in South America, land of the Chibchas; but she herself had no indigenous mix. Her two daughters were the same way.

One day, Berni—still himself, but also that "other" self—left early on a day off when he was supposed to be at home watching the baby. He took the baby and went to the sitter's house, and handing her the child, said: "Good morning, ma'am. Today I'm not only leaving Marco Antonio with you, I'm staying too so you can take care of us both." The lady burst into laughter and, as best she could, took the baby but told him, "Don Berni, the child stays, but you are going straight back the way you came."

"Oh, no, ma'am. Please let me stay here with you, because I have the day off and my wife went to work. Besides—listen—I can't be alone at home because I'm afraid of loneliness."

"Ha! I'm sorry, but I don't believe a word of that." And with that, she shut the door in his face.

Berni kept being the same. That other self—the one that always hounded him when he was in front of a woman, and a beautiful one at that.

The phone rang. A distant voice.

Chapter 9
Crossroads in Miami

"Me, Berni. Who's there?"

"It's me, brother—Arge. I'm calling from Buenaventura. Please, Berni, find out where, when, and why my son—the Chubby One—was detained!"

"What—my God—who told you such a thing?" Berni asked.

"He called me, but I couldn't understand where he was; the clearest thing was that he was in jail."

"Okay, brother. Calm down and tell me more slowly what you gathered."

Arge had little or no further information. Berni promised to call back in three hours and asked him not to move from the phone.

Berni set about calling every person, office, friend—anywhere that might have news of Fernel. Five hours later, he was able to reach the wife of a man who, many years earlier, had driven one of Arge's trucks. Her husband couldn't speak. She was crying, her voice shaking with fear one moment and rage the next. Berni managed to make out that both of them were in the custody of the FBI in Los Angeles, accused of drug trafficking, and that the judge would read out the charges the next day. She had eight children in a row and, when she left with Fernel, she had just started building her own auto-mechanic business.

Berni immediately called his brother in Buenaventura and told him everything. "Wait for more news from me tomorrow and every day until this is over. I don't know how much bail they'll set for the two of them, but I won't lie to you: it's very unlikely they'll be granted it. It's up to the judge's discretion—and when it comes to Colombians, His Honor seems to lose his discretion."

"Hello? Hello?" Berni shouted, thinking the line had dropped.

"Yes... yes," Arge said, and couldn't speak another word.

Berni kept his brother informed of every development. But he didn't tell him directly and bluntly that there was no point in hiring a lawyer—he couldn't crush his hope that his son might be released. Berni knew the justice system of the United States was one of the best in the world, but for Colombians accused of drug trafficking and its related aggravating offenses, things were priced differently. That is: a Colombian charged with drug trafficking who can't present clear evidence of lawful employment at the moment of arrest is not a trustworthy person for any judge. He told all this to Lilian, rather than to his brother, Fernel's father. In almost those same words, the judge who heard the appeal filed by a lawyer for Fernel confirmed the ruling. In these cases, the lawyers are more like bystanders than protagonists; what decides things are facts the court deems "reliable."

Berni loved his brother and all his brother's children—among them the Chubby One, as everyone called him. He was super-special, with a natural charm. It's strange how people don't tend to heed warnings from others, and Berni had warned him about what could happen.

Berni and Lilian went to visit the Sacred Heart of Jesus to give thanks for the help in resisting the temptation to go with Fernel to Los Angeles—for it hadn't been easy, not only because of the bond between them but because the money was there in Chubby's house, ready to arrive and be scooped up. It wasn't true.

In Arge's household—the third child of Doña Carmen and Don Marcos, who might one day have been named by Rome's College of Cardinals as the Holy Father of the Catholics—not because he was a saint, but because he was the son of a saint, for his intelligence, and because he was born in Colombia's Miracle City, which should have guaranteed he'd work miracles—there was no more laughter. In that home on the Isla del Cascajal, everyone moved about like robots, not knowing how, or why, or when the tragedy had happened. It was a living death. Something like being buried alive. Arge, Fernel's father, hadn't been wrong when he said he had a feeling he would never see his beloved Gordito again. And so it was.

There was sadness in Berni's home, too. His children had gone to live in Miami, and he had a very bad feeling. Something was going to happen.

The best of all the bad that was on its way was the news that, in the darkness of prison, Fernel was looking for God and had dedicated himself to studying the Bible. He did indeed find Him—and it wasn't hard, because extremes meet. It seemed he began to work miracles among the prison population, and it could be true: like his father, he'd been born in Colombia's Miracle City. But the power of the spirit he claimed to have as a gift from God didn't help him heal his mother, who died first; nor, eight years later, his father, who died in his sickbed without ever seeing his Gordito free.

In phone conversations between Berni and Fernel from prison, Chubby said he had baptized his father and that he'd gotten up from bed completely cured—though he got up to go to the notary to legalize the will leaving his estate to his daughter, the only one who truly deserved all the property and money Arge would leave. She was the only one who always helped her father and stood by him through good times and bad. She was the only one who didn't emigrate with her mother when she and the other children left him in dire financial straits many years before he was arrested. When Fernel learned of this, he flew into a rage and began railing against his father and siblings. Berni reminded him one day that the words he used, demanding his share of the estate, contradicted the Lord's words to the young man who wished to convert and follow Him: "Leave everything and follow me."

Chubby left prison scarcely a year after his father's death, and while founding a Christian church to teach people to leave everything and follow Christ, he took control of all his father's assets. In a single year back on the Isla del Cascajal, he already had two 50-ton semi-trailers, the transport agency, the buildings and the parcel of land they stood on, family vehicles, furniture, and bank accounts. He declared himself the universal heir to the probated estate, and the will that had legal force, naming his younger sister as heir—she herself tore it up, because she had no interest in material things. Her brother had taught her that true wealth, the only kind that brings happiness, is spiritual wealth. She obeyed.

Berni went to Colombia to visit Gordo and fulfill their promise: that together—with a bottle of aguardiente between chest and back—they would cry until they drowned in tears. That was what they had agreed during a phone call from the federal building in El Paso, Texas, where Chubby had spent "some months" in custody. Berni expected him to be the same as always, but he was wrong. Fernel wouldn't go drink with him anywhere. He was a teetotaler. Berni tried to persuade him and couldn't. He tried to stir his feelings—his old calling card—to get him to cry naturally, without stimulants, and couldn't. Berni took leave of that cold, unscrupulous, ungrateful, strange "new Christian," a peculiar son of Christ who would never again drink aguardiente so as not to offend God.

Berni loved God in a different way, and he went off with his wife Lilian—by then already devoted to one another—to drink aguardiente, to cry over Arge's death, over the death of friendship, and of Chubby's old vices, to toast the wealth of Christians, of pastors, of priests, to toast life, love, and happiness. In the country place where Berni and his wife were, they knew him very well, and when they saw him crying so much, they asked Lilian why she was weeping like that. She told them her feelings were in pieces because, after Berni had come all the way from the United States, Chubby hadn't gone with him to mourn his brother.

When Amado and his wife, the owners of the rustic venue on the slopes of Dapa on the outskirts of Cali, heard this, they told them not to worry, that at any moment he'd show up—because "he always comes to drink here; he prefers this place where no one knows him."

"Are you sure?" Berni asked, stopping his crying.

"Yes, it's true—just two days ago he was here, he got drunk, and went off to a motel."

Berni burst into laughter and, raising his glass, toasted to the Chubby One's health.

In Miami, Berni's children and his ex-wife were living once again. With a few dollars, they managed to buy a home. A close Peruvian friend, familiar with the purchase procedures, helped with the deal.

But suddenly, and under the care of doctors at the Children's Hospital, the son of Berni and María began to show health problems. The doctors were surprised by the setback they were seeing in Alberto. Three years in New Jersey had affected him greatly. Twelve years earlier, his parents had walked proudly out of the Chayo Clinic in Bogotá after one of the best open-heart surgeries ever performed there.

Meanwhile, Berni began trying to convince Lilian to move back to Miami despite their bad first experience living there. "We need to be close to my children for when they need us," he told Lilian—who already knew all about Alberto's treatment, since she had often taken him to his hospital appointments.

"All right, let's go," she said. "But we need to start getting everything ready." Lilian had a special affection for Berni's children, but at that very moment, her mother was living in their apartment. When Lilian proposed the move, her mother refused and chose to stay in her son's apartment. Berni was aware of how painful that goodbye would be, but he also knew the situation Berni himself was going through.

After they agreed, Berni called his son in Miami and promised that by the next birthday, in March, they would be together again. Alberto was happy.

In the early hours of January 30, everything was quiet and people were asleep, but Lilian—who slept with her ears beyond the walls— heard someone calling for Berni. She looked out and saw, down on the sidewalk by the front door, a friend of Berni's—the same man who had sold him a car mid-flight to Colombia. Lilian woke Berni, and he tossed the front-door key down in a plastic bag.

"Brother," the friend said, "they called me at 6 a.m. at my apartment because your phone wouldn't pick up. Your daughter says they've been calling you from Miami since dawn. Your son Alberto has died."

Berni had quit smoking when his son Marco Antonio was born, but without realizing it, he found himself smoking and crying.

After a shower—only half as long as the ones he usually took, because his body was trembling—Berni left with his friend Gustavo. He had never been seen to tremble, not even when he stood in front of a bull during one of the festivals in Lomitas, the town where his parents had once lived in retirement. Not even hemophilia had kept him, along with Fernel, from making a few passes at the animal. At the travel agency, recognizing the emergency, they issued the tickets; since his friend could not go with him, Berni asked his sister to go in his place.

Berni was inconsolable on the flight, and together with his sister—the most tearful woman in the world—they flooded the plane. He told her that the night before, he had spoken with his son, and the boy had promised to wait so they could celebrate his next birthday together.

He passed away at Miami Children's Hospital, under the care of heart specialists, listed for a transplant, and after undergoing surgery at the best clinic in the Americas, Chayo in Bogotá. His parents did everything within their power.

Family members and capable attorneys, aware of the situation, recommended filing a lawsuit against everyone involved, as the Colombian saying goes. However, Latin romanticism prevailed—perhaps a lack of ambition—and the parents' consolation lay in the fact that money could not bring their beloved son back. The school honored him posthumously with a high school diploma.

These events hastened Berni and his family's return to Miami. They left the doors open in New York, but Lilian's mother refused to live in Miami. Berni went ahead, driving his car. A month later, after saving up for the apartment deposit and the cost of moving their furniture, he went to pick up Lilian and their son.

A new chapter began. Berni had his papers in order, including his divorce. His children were now just a 15-minute drive away. The apartment they moved into was next to the one his brother Jaime occupied. Across the hall lived his sisters, Libertad and Luzmila; even his eldest sister, Lucila, the pharmacy owner, had come to Miami as a tourist, hoping to open a business. Everything seemed set for happiness, that elusive happiness everyone chases.

In their homes and apartments, people came and went. No one was happier than Berni. Jaime and Berni organized spectacular birthday parties and Halloweens—the "witches' party," called pagan by prudish women who don't drink or don't know how to dance. The "holy" parties began at eight in the evening and lasted until the next morning. That's how Colombians celebrate. Their parties never ended—they continued the next day, the next week, or whenever.

One night, the police arrived—someone had dialed 911—after a neighbor complained about the loud music and the clanging of the frog-toss game, whose brass rings made a loud chime when they hit the bronze frog. Each player got six throws, and that night, more than twelve people lined up. The chiming sounded every minute. The game started at six in the evening; by midnight, it was still going strong. Jaime, Berni, and their sisters—with the same kindness, respect, and conviction their mother Doña Carmen had used when convincing others to help those in need—gradually won over the two officers. Without realizing it, the officers picked up the rings and began trying to toss them into the frog's mouth, "just to get one in," they eagerly said. They left at dawn, only after one of them finally scored. "Wonderful game," they said as they left.

The next day, during a family council, they decided that not only did they have the right to have fun—but the whole neighborhood did. They sent invitation cards to all the neighbors. "This is the Bermuda Triangle," Berni joked. "If we're lost, it's only natural for everyone else to get lost too." At later parties, you could see Colombians, Cubans, Puerto Ricans, Nicaraguans, Dominicans, Mexicans, Haitians, Venezuelans, Argentines, Brazilians, and the occasional European or Westerner. The crowd grew: some were Catholic, others Evangelical or Christian, and others of different religions—sharing the same God. Democrats and Republicans—there were no religious, political, or economic differences among them. "Just as you see all these people gathered here, happy and united, without prejudice—that's how the world should be, my dear friend Manuel," Berni told his closest friend, a Bogotano nicknamed "Chino." Manuel—though not "simple," as Berni liked to joke—

147

was incredibly intelligent. Strangely, he had joined a religious sect. That didn't matter; they loved everyone equally.

But more than love, friendship, and happiness, envy and anger prevailed. One morning, after a night of partying, Berni woke to find his apartment empty. Lilian—his secretary, lover, companion, and the mother of his son—had slipped away at dawn. Worst of all, she had taken their son, Marco Antonio, who was only three years old. Lilian was the same woman who had once called the police. Berni had been sleeping with the enemy. After several hours of inquiries, Berni learned that Lilian was already in New York—to stay, forever.

Like anyone else, Berni could no longer keep it together at the office, and his performance began to decline.

Arge, his brother, heard of the situation through third parties and called from the Isla del Cascajal to invite him to come work with him. "I need you, brother. Come here and I'll make you manager. I'll transfer all my powers to you," Arge said. "I'm old and tired, and I need someone responsible like you." Berni thanked him for the offer but declined, assuring Arge that if Lilian didn't return within a month, he would likely travel there after a phone call. "All right, little brother. I love you," Arge said, before hanging up.

Two weeks later, the phone rang. A hoarse, nervous voice spoke on the other end. "Berni, if you want to see me again, you have to come live here in New York." It was Lilian's voice. "Hi, Lilian—how is my son?" "He's fine," she replied. "But listen to me. If you want to be with me, to give me the happiness of being close to my son—raising him, helping him, educating him—you can come back. The doors of the house are open." "Which house?" Berni asked. "I've rented a house for us. My family has moved out; now it's just the two of us."

In fact, Berni wasn't lying. Everyone had moved: Jaime to Miami Lakes, Luzmila to New Jersey, Lucila back to Colombia, and Libertad moved in with Luzmila. The Bermuda Triangle had disappeared. A few days before the end of November, Hurricane Lilian devastated the place where the triangle had stood. It was left desolate, and the neighbors returned to their old, monotonous, boring lives. The area was once again filled with people glued to their chairs, watching canned soap operas on TV.

Berni was clear with Lilian, and she agreed—but with conditions. He promised to give up liquor and work harder. It was hard for him, but he did it, thinking of his son and what he had already lost—again—because of excess drinking and dancing. "The load gets adjusted along the way," as the muleteer says when the journey begins. Lilian got what she wanted—Berni gave up drinking—and he, in turn, succeeded in getting back his beloved Marco Antonio. Two days later, Berni hugged his son and Lilian at Miami International Airport.

Phone calls with Arge, Berni's brother, became more frequent and interesting. On one occasion, they talked about Fernel's desire to convert Arge—his father—to Christianity, which, according to Fernel, was necessary for healing from the terminal illness that led to his death. Meanwhile, doctors were trying to save him. Fernel's proposal seemed more advantageous because, as the pastors say, when healing is achieved, the soul is healed too, and one earns eternal life. "Hmm. A two-for-one," Berni said. "That's a double play." "Nonsense," Arge replied. "My son has nothing to teach me about religion, and as for my body, it's more here than there. The flesh doesn't matter." "All right, little brother," Berni said, "but don't forget your son wants you alive." "Alive? I've been dead since the day I was arrested," Arge replied. "Okay—talk later, little brother," Berni said. "See you soon."

Christianity was sweeping through Catholics in Colombia, particularly on the Isla del Cascajal—within Arge's family. Only Arge and Gabriel, another of his sons, were spared. "It's a big, delicate dilemma," Berni told Lilian when they discussed the subject. They had been spared conversion, but according to the Christians, they wouldn't be spared divine judgment. A chubby, converted pastor arrived on the island, gathered his flock, and set out in search of salvation for everyone. "God is the only one who can save the soul," Berni said. "But if someone else helps, it seems praiseworthy to me. Right, Mrs. Lilian?" "What needs to be done," she answered, "is for each one to save their own."

I believe that if anyone could save a soul and turn it into a pure spirit, it was my brother Argemiro. He was one of the most Catholic men ever to walk this planet—except for a few Popes of the Church. Only because of a mistake by his mother, Doña Carmen, and Don Marco, he did not become the Holy Father of Christendom. Had he become it, we wouldn't have to work—we'd all be kept, even in Mercedes-Benzes.

Had I known what I know today, I would have sued the entire Jesuit congregation of France, Rome, and Spain—even the convents in this country—and the Jesuit convent in Popayán, where it was believed some Jesuits had come from the Iberian Peninsula, bringing with them that vice of homosexuality.

The one who saved her soul was Doña Carmen—through her love of the Sacred Heart of Jesus, her deep compassion for her neighbor, and her unwavering kindness to everyone in need. Yet, she wasn't spared another tragedy. She had barely finished mourning the death of her son Gustavo when she was notified of the death of her son Adalberto, the third of eleven children. Adalberto, the one who once tried to stop a ship weighing over 10,000 tons with his foot to prevent it from colliding with the edge of a wall at the port of Buenaventura, was a pilot working for the Buenaventura Port Authority. He had died the day before from a cardiac arrest in the Miracle City—Armenia, Quindío, the world's coffee capital.

Adalberto, the second-born of the family, had passed just 16 days ago, and Arge's favorite brother was still on his spiritual quest, seeking God. He had been saving his soul, having been in purgatory for more than 30 years—enough time to place him at the top of the soul-saving list. After all, the soul-saving lists move faster than the U.S. immigration lists.

The situation is clear. Arge loved Adalberto as a son, and Adalberto, in turn, loved Arge as his brother. When Arge died, his spirit visited Adalberto and invited him to join him. Adalberto eagerly accepted. Then, Arge interceded before God, and the Almighty skipped his turn, placing him at the top of the list. As Adalberto's heart weakened, two weeks passed between the two deaths. This was expected because Adalberto had lost his three children—not because he was a bad father like Bemi, but because they had made poor choices.

Before his death, Adalberto visited the Miracle City with his wife, where he performed the miracle of reuniting his children on Mother's Day—the greatest celebration in Colombia after Christmas. He forgave them, handing each one the key to his house so they could visit him. "Don't do it for me," he said. "Do it for your mother, who loves you more than I do."

Meanwhile, Jaime would be the only one of Carmen's children to end up in a U.S. federal prison on charges of possession and trafficking of heroin, many years after his mother's passing. The drug trade was wreaking havoc in Colombia, and the allure of money from distributing it reached Jaime. Despite his sharp instinct for risk, he failed to detect the danger in time and was caught at the Miami airport with cocaine.

Banks, of course, would never disclose information about the global drug trade. The situation resembled what happens in the circus when the dwarf grows taller. They couldn't fire him because everyone liked him, so they decided to keep him and hoped that by pairing him with another dwarf, they could produce a normal-sized child.

Berni thought about this, but he kept it to himself, not wanting to scandalize his visitors.

The Gomez family continued to face challenges. Luzmila, still young, developed a severe illness in her right kidney. As she said, had it been the left one, her family would have refused to help. Every two days, the doctor had to perform dialysis. Fortunately, the insurance covered it, or she would have died. Of her four children, only her daughter could have helped her.

Berni and Arge had frequent conversations before Arge's death—not only because of their shared interests but because, with age, comes nostalgia. Reminiscing about the past offered a way to cope with it. They discussed love, betrayal, women, war, peace, religion, and much more. They had plenty to talk about, and they did so with insight.

Arge remarked about the guerrillas: "They now have economic power, and just when they could have had political power, they no longer care. They aren't interested in peace agreements because it would be inconvenient now that they're linked to drug cartel leaders, even those in prison. Moreover, they get their weapons through Russian leaders, who still hold the political and economic power of the former Soviet Union."

Berni responded, "I think, for peace, we must concede the territory they demand, but the Colombian government should not allow them to govern it."

One day, they went to one of the most elegant restaurants in the city. Afterward, they returned home because Arge wasn't feeling well—he was showing signs of a serious medical condition. The doctor had advised him against drinking alcohol. Berni tried to convince him to join him for drinks and a walk around the city, but all his attempts were in vain.

The next day, Berni traveled to Cali to visit Jaime, who was on vacation before his arrest in Miami for carrying just under a pound of heroin. Jaime had a surprise for Berni. He had organized a welcome party and, more importantly, introduced him to a woman he had known from childhood. They had played together in the city of Miracles when they were young.

The woman was beautiful, with ideal measurements and a smile worth millions. Berni was amazed and felt it was a gift from providence. After a few drinks, he dared to propose they finish the game they had started in their youth. She agreed, saying she had been waiting for this moment for a long time.

But then, in an unexpected turn of events, Berni fell critically ill. He suffered an intestinal rupture, and being a hemophiliac, he bled heavily. He was rushed to the hospital in Miami, and what was supposed to be a brief vacation turned into an emergency hospital stay. He survived, saved by divine intervention, just as he had been when he was a child.

In letters his brothers Jaime and Arge would later receive, Berni begged them to be very careful, as hemophilia was a dangerous and treacherous condition that could ruin their best plans.

This event in Berni's life forced him to take radical measures regarding alcohol and sexual relations. He gave up everything, except relationships. He would never give those up.

He expressed this in a letter to his brother Arge some time after leaving the hospital.

"My dear heir to the monarchies," said Berni's doctor in a slow tone, "you can never drink your little aguardiente, smoke, or engage in intense activities like playing soccer anymore. Your diet should be plain, and no citrus liquids." Berni remembered the doctor's words from over 37 years ago when he had been in a similar condition.

Berni had to live a new life. Two things worried him greatly: one was the risk of contracting AIDS due to blood transfusions, and the other was the staggering hospital bill, which amounted to $55,000.00 for just six days of hospitalization. The pleas of Doña Carmen, his wives' requests, the demands from his children—none of it had been enough to make Berni stop drinking. But now, Berni was determined to change his lifestyle and dedicate more time to studying English, with the aim of obtaining naturalization. In the coming months, he would become an American citizen, and he did, in a grand ceremony the following July. His wife, Maria Mercedes, also became a citizen. On this day, they concluded that each would be independent of the other, and things didn't go as she had hoped.

As a result of these changes, Berni managed to gather enough money to purchase a new home by making a down payment. He believed Lilian and her son deserved it, as he was the best student at the schools he attended, and she was a woman of great character. The salary he received from an exploitative company wouldn't have been enough to even consider buying a house, but the money he received from Princess Diana of England was.

Berni did not receive the money directly from the British crown, but in an indirect way. A café had opened in Coconut Grove with an attraction—a tunnel that could be traversed at 90 miles per hour in a simulator capsule. Berni worked in a parking lot just a few blocks away and was invited to the café's opening. Berni came up with an idea to earn extra money without robbing anyone, as that would go against the clear examples left by his father, Don Marcos. He proposed to the café manager that he pay him $2 for each tourist or person who came to the café in his name. Thousands of cards with Berni's name were printed, and every day, about 100 tourists would arrive at the parking lot where Berni worked. After assisting them, he would give them the card and tell them that they could visit the tunnel where Lady Diana had had her accident with her lover. Tourists' curiosity was boundless, and the lines to enter the café were endless. Every day, Berni would collect $200, and he ended up accumulating thousands of dollars. "Truly," Berni would say to his friends and family, "the little princess was the best representative of the United Kingdom to her people and the other peoples of the world. Had the Europeans not packed their bags and left, Berni would be a millionaire today, a true heir to royalty."

On another trip to Colombia to visit his family and brothers, Berni sat down to talk with his favorite brother, Arge. Before his death, Arge expressed his concern about his children and grandchildren converting to Christianity. According to Fernel, Arge's son wanted to baptize him again. Arge told Berni that his daughter, the person he loved most, now saw him as a stranger, as if he were no longer her father.

Chapter 10
The Vigil at the Hospital

"Well, brother," Berni replied, "what's happening is that you are doubting your faith, which is why you are afraid of the arrival of your son-pastor, and you are distancing yourself from your beloved daughter to avoid the issue. Don't be afraid, because all they've done is change religion; their faith and love for God are still the same as yours. Nothing changes. Their foundation is the word of God written in your Bible. What they are experiencing is just a new guide. I don't know who will be your guide here, but I know that your son's guide there is none other than Mr. Cplan, one of the most famous pastors in North America. The issue with religions is about rebellion, a protest against certain parameters. Deep down, we are all loving the same God, who changes name according to regions, cultures, and times. As for faith, it's the same. Welcome your son when he returns, listen to him, and let him keep his faith, now dressed in Christianity. Talk to your daughter, listen to her, and accept her with her new outfit. She was always good, and now she feels pure. Wonderful. Muslims, Jews, Catholics, Christians in all their different divisions, we are all seeking salvation. This is the key. But of all these trends, the most important is love. I believe, my distinguished ex-student of the Marista school," Berni concluded, "No religion can divide parents and children. Let money be the one to do that."

"And from here, you know how to handle such a delicate issue as religion," Arge said.

"Well, my dear brother," Berni said, standing up, "what happens is that you are losing your memory. I received my first knowledge from you. Do you remember our father's wake? On the other hand," Berni continued without waiting for a response, "I have studied the Bible, and I found that there's room for all of us; and, in the United States, only religion is known, just like here there is only violence, in Cuba, socialism, and in Argentina, soccer. Finally, let me tell you, when you reach my age, you know almost everything, or you don't live anymore."

"Almost everything?" Arge asked. "Why almost everything?"

"Well, not everything," Berni said. "If I knew women, I would know everything."

Both laughed heartily and shook hands in agreement. They both knew hundreds of women, but they didn't really know them as they truly were.

Berni spent delightful moments with his brother, and now that they weren't drinking, they could discuss more about economics, politics, and religion, but less about sex and women, since it was through alcohol that they made their great conquests.

Once back in Miami, Berni returned to his work. The lot of land had been used for parking operations. Some employees from nearby businesses, as well as tourists, were Berni's customers. On rare occasions, contractors would park there. One day, Berni was attending the parking lot on a cool early January day when a man arrived, paid for parking, and went to park his vehicle, which was a closed vehicle used by people transporting materials. The man spoke to Berni as if he had known him before.

"You must be Cuban, right?" Berni asked the newcomer.

"Yes, I was born in Havana," the man replied. "And you, you're Colombian, right?"

"Yes, sir," Berni said, smiling. "Where's the cocaine?"

"No, sir, I don't sell it."

"Strange, since you're Colombian."

"And tell me, why does this guy César Gaviria want Fidel to help free his brother, who was kidnapped by the communists in your country? Can you explain that?"

156

Berni, surprised by the man's confidence and directness, took a breath and answered slowly: "First, let me tell you, it's easier for a Cuban to sell cocaine than for a Colombian because my countrymen have transferred the business to your countrymen to avoid the relentless police persecution. You may not have much information about this. Second, that César Gaviria is a respectable former president of Colombia, who, because of his honesty and knowledge of the state, was chosen as the Secretary of the Organization of American States. In the good romance of the Spanish language, this would be like being the Secretary of State of the United States. This honorable and excellent man asked Mr. Fidel Castro for help to convince the guerrillas—speaking in their dialect—to release his brother. And so, the Gaviria family was able to have their son back at home—a respectable Colombian."

"Anyway, dear sir, when you need to educate yourself, come by here, and I will gladly help you."

The visitor began walking away, muttering aloud that he would continue the conversation on his way back because he was being called to estimate some repairs.

An hour later, the man returned and resumed the conversation, asking Berni why Colombians were allowing their country to be overtaken by communists. Berni sat down in his chair and began his response: "Well, sir, what's your name?"

"Roberto," the man replied.

"Ah, well, Mr. Roberto," Berni said, "in my country, there are fewer communists than here. And if what you're suggesting is that the Colombian guerrillas are communists, I'll tell you that they include communists, liberals, conservatives, socialists, environmentalists, religious people, and power-hungry fanatics—not just for economic power, but political power too. Lately, there are also drug dealers and coca growers among them. The thing is, they are all united by one goal: to create repression against the government to force it to meet social demands. On the other hand, in Cuba, your beloved Cuba, Mr. Fidel Castro's government uses the army of gendarmes to repress the people and force them into social programs."

Roberto approached Berni and asked, "You're a communist, right?"

Berni laughed and said, "I'm not a communist, but you sure are a Cuban-ism."

Berni continued, "For the Cuban diaspora, anyone who doesn't agree with their views is a communist."

"And what is the diaspora?" Roberto asked.

"Hmm, better let me go get my card because it's time for me to leave," Berni replied. "When I return, I'll explain to you what the diaspora is."

Berni had met hundreds of thousands of people who came to the parking lot where he worked for three years. He talked to everyone, especially tourists from around the world—Spaniards, who remained as foolish as ever, Germans, who now had the chance to clone and purify the race, Russians, who shared state property like the Nicaraguans once did, and Latinos—lots of tourism, much tourism.

When the lot was empty, Berni had time to write, and some of his articles were sent to the best newspaper in Miami, where a few were published. The others weren't because they had to make space for other stories. The press had to set an example of democracy, even if the other articles weren't better.

When the people of the United States elected a Democrat, William Jefferson Clinton, Berni wrote to recommend several revolutionary reforms for education, health, and social welfare systems, based on Oscar Wilde's classic story "The Happy Prince." The President replied, thanking him for his ideas in search of a new world order for the new millennium.

But the son of Doña Carmen, born in the most miraculous city in the world, on same day as the birth of Jesus, an advanced student at the universities of Cali, Colombia, an English student at MDCC in Miami, a naturalized American citizen, the best employee at a parking management firm, and the friendliest Colombian—heir by descent of his mother's royal lineage—was the only employee on Earth who had nowhere to sleep.

One cold December afternoon, he waited until no one was around and went between the cars to urinate. The parking lot was full of cars. When he finished, he put his equipment back in place and was about to return to his work. At that moment, a car honked its horn— it was the same car he had just urinated on. He looked inside and saw the owner, a bank executive. The respectable lady called him over. When Berni approached, before she could say anything, he immediately offered his apologies, his face burning with embarrassment, his blood rushing to his head. She, with a Mona Lisa smile, accepted his apology and said she had observed everything. "Don't worry, you're privileged. Congratulations."

Berni had never felt fear before. First, because he knew the strong laws against public exposure of sexual organs; second, because the client was a respectable and distinguished lady, and his bosses were very strict. On top of that, the worst part was that he had no witnesses to prove there was no malice in his actions. Berni sat there, waiting for the large delegation that would come to fire him from his job. He was sure that would happen, despite the lady's attitude.

Later that afternoon, Berni went home and told his wife Lilian and son everything. "I think," he said, "I'll be fired tomorrow. I'm sorry."

The next day, Berni waited for his boss or the management team to arrive. At 8 a.m., a car stopped in front of his booth. The lady driving it was the same one from the previous day. She lowered the car window, looked at him, and slowly said, "Good morning, Berni, how are you doing?" Then she continued to her parking space and parked her car. From that day forward, she would stop to greet him every day, something she had never done before. Berni called her the "Mona Lisa" because of her delicate smile.

Lucila, the noblewoman, was running her drugstore business again in the city of Señora. Her life had changed, but not enough to make her miserable. She was with a 70-year-old man, but she still had the energy—or the "little bomb"—needed to attend to a wife.

However, the only man who could fulfill all Lucila's needs was Ernesto, and it was important that his name was Ernesto. The problem with him was that he had been liberal and foolish, like few liberals. He could have changed parties and married the best woman of the time. Surely, Don Marcos would have accepted him into his home and given him his daughter. After all, if he was so tough and so liberal, after marriage, he could have returned to the conservative camp as if nothing had happened. If a truck can overturn with 50,000 eggs, why can't a man with two? Lucila's children from her first marriage opposed this, but the illustrious Mr. Ernesto demonstrated that his interest in her was purely sexual. When he realized the comments, he renounced all rights to Lucila's property in a public deed, and thus, he left it documented when she passed away some years later.

Luzmila, the blue-eyed girl who had been deceived by a man who raped her without ever loving her, continued her struggle to live, enduring her kidney disease stoically. In her phone conversations with her family, she expressed her tiredness but never showed a desire to die. She wanted to live but wasn't willing to undergo the treatment to keep her alive.

Miryam, the skinny one who should have changed her name to Freedom, moved to Miami to escape the cold of New York. She had entered her 70s. Only fools stay in the North after that age when the cold seeps into the bones and reaches the brain.

Berni frequently visited her apartment in a housing complex in Kendall. One day, she gave him the exciting news that Lilia, Doña Carmen's youngest daughter, who once married a man claiming to own a property at the foot of Vijes, near Cali, would soon arrive with her entire family—her husband, her eldest daughter, and the two men of the marriage. They would meet her daughter in Miami, "my doll," as they always called Sherley. Sherley, a beautiful young woman, had arrived earlier, engaged to an American man who soon separated from her because, despite being 30 years old, he was still under the control of his mother.

Miryam and Berni shared a strong, brotherly relationship, and she confided in him about all her troubles. She often joked about wanting to be in the Guinness Book of World Records as the mother of all lamentations. She could turn a glass of water into a storm and cry longer than Doña Carmen, who wept for five continuous years after her son Gustavo died in a motorcycle accident at the age of 25. Miryam would look out of her apartment window and cry when the day was dark and threatening a storm. The next day, if the sun shone brightly and the sky was blue, she would burst into tears, thanking God for the beauty of the weather and life. She cried for others' tragedies as if they were her own. Her emotions were like layers of an onion—each layer, a different feeling. She wept more than the mothers of young men murdered during Pinochet's dictatorship or the mothers of those kidnapped by Colombia's guerrillas.

When Berni learned that his sister Lilia would be arriving from Colombia, thanks to the visas granted by the U.S. Embassy, he consulted with Miryam about inviting them for dinner. She advised him to be careful, recalling an incident when she had invited her son for dinner that ended in disaster.

"How? What happened? Which of your children are you talking about?" Berni asked, intrigued as he was unaware of the issue.

Miryam replied, "Berni, let me tell you. My son Juan promised never to come back to our house again because of what happened the last time you invited him to dinner. That day, he was treated very well, but during the meal, he noticed there were no ripe fried plantain slices. We didn't serve them, which is a traditional custom in Colombian cooking. It's his favorite dish because I always make them for him."

"I'm sorry, my dear sister, but the truth is, after ten years of living here, I've lost some of the traditions from home. I assure you, this won't happen again." Berni went home and immediately ordered his wife, also Colombian, not to forget to make fried ripe plantains for dinner, realizing it was a serious mistake not to serve them when hosting a guest. "We need to be careful," Berni told her. "In a few days, my sister Lilia will arrive, and we're going to invite her and her family to dinner."

The Gomez family had endured many challenges, and Berni reflected on the past. "For your information," he told Miryam, "because of a mistake my mother made, my father committed suicide, despite Doña Carmen offering the most ceremonial apologies. My older brother, the firstborn, also committed suicide because his wife prevented him from attending a birthday party. No one knows if my nephew will ever forgive us for the offense he suffered in this house. May Christ save us."

From that point on, Lilia was careful not to make any mistakes that would affect her relationship with Berni. She realized that they weren't like other people who simply endured life's ups and downs.

One day, Lilia asked Berni if he loved her with all his heart, and he responded, "The heart is just an organ that pumps blood throughout the body. It's responsible for nourishing every part of you. But love, Lilia, is an attitude—an emotion one person has toward another. It can be unreciprocated. It's feelings like pity, tolerance, anxiety, and passion. If love were based solely on the heart, it wouldn't end until death, or until the heart stops beating. But when romantics talk about love, they're speaking about what feeds people's sensitivity."

"Ah," said Lilia, "Then how do you explain the great pain in the heart when a man is unfaithful to his wife?"

Berni responded, "It's not pain in the heart—it's the reaction to bruised pride, the offense to respect and the person. It's the pressure on the chest that comes with impotence."

Lilia reflected on the conversation in deep silence, remembering how sensitive the Gomez family was. Berni, thinking about what his beloved sister had said, reassured her: "Don't worry about infidelities, because I'm blind. I no longer see other women." This comforted Berni's wife, who had never truly trusted him.

The next week, Marcello, a student from Kendall School, went on vacation. His father had promised him a trip to New York if he brought home grades of A- or A, so he asked his father to pack his bags. Berni confessed that, having changed companies the previous month, he couldn't accompany him on the trip. But if his mom agreed to go with him, he'd have no problem buying the tickets. Lilia agreed to go, not only because she had a special attraction to New York, the capital of the world, but because she now had full trust in her new husband—new because Berni had changed significantly. He no longer drank, smoked, or was unfaithful. He worked hard and made love to her, just as every woman liked. She had never been so trusting, leaving him alone at home. Two days later, Berni waved goodbye from the roof of the Miami airport building, where he went up to watch the plane take off, carrying his son and wife.

Colombians have a saying: "The gentleman repeats himself."

And Berni was indeed a gentleman in every sense of the word. Less than 24 hours after Lilia left, Berni already had a date with a friend. They went out to clubs all night, and when Berni realized that everything was going well and that he was beginning to miss his beloved wife, he confided in his companion. "My wife and son are on vacation in New York, and I suffer from panic in solitude. Tonight, I won't be able to sleep. I'll have the most terrible moments of my life." The lady believed him.

When she accepted what he said, she lowered her head so she wouldn't notice his mask. But her response wasn't what Berni had hoped. She told him she couldn't stay because she hadn't prepared to be away from home and hadn't informed her parents she was coming back the next day. Berni tried again, but the meeting never took place. He spent that night in utter despair. The alcohol, which he wasn't used to anymore, made him sick and dizzy. He spent more time with his head in the toilet than in bed. He couldn't eat anything because, despite trying to recover, nothing stayed in his stomach. He called her and begged her to come over and take care of him, but she replied she had too much work to leave the office.

"How ridiculous this country makes women," Berni thought. "They give priority to work, leaving sex for later." He fell asleep, waiting for a call that never came. He slept until the next day.

Five days later, Berni called another friend, Penelope, who agreed to let him come over. On the way, he bought a dozen red roses and a bottle of Cristal aguardiente, a liquor she had mentioned she'd never had before. This time, Berni drank with discretion, especially because he was at her apartment. They danced and toasted to the good things in life. She was a beautiful woman—natural and pleasant, a quality Puerto Rican women possess. They danced to three songs from the CD when Berni suddenly felt the absence of his wife. She noticed. "What do we do?" she asked. "Let's go to bed," he said. "Wait a few minutes while I take my son—he's 2 years old—to my neighbor."

Berni sat and waited, but she returned with the child in hand. "Let me go to my friend's house on the lower floor," she said. Ten minutes passed, and she returned with the child. "Don't worry, my friend is on the other floor, and she's back," she said. The friend couldn't take the child because she was going out with her husband for dinner. Penelope returned half an hour later, but by then, Berni had already forgotten about his wife. He was deeply asleep. She woke him up, told him to go home, and promised not to leave him uninspired next time.

Berni went to his car, started it, and headed home. On the way, he thought the forces of evil were against him because strange things were happening.

The next day, he sat down to read a classic storybook published by Editorial América S.A. in 1991 and continued with the story "The Raven King." When he finished, he reflected on how difficult it was to have sex in the United States. Women worked on the streets, then came home to work and fall asleep from exhaustion. And those who didn't work couldn't do it either because they had to care for their children. "What wonderful moments those were with my wife when she was my lover," Berni thought. He realized those moments, full of passion, wouldn't return. He glanced at the clock and realized his family would soon be back from their trip. It was Saturday afternoon, a good day for love, but would it still feel the same? Berni concluded that Lilia no longer undressed or jumped into bed like playful cats. She demanded the lights off, the doors and curtains closed. "At what point did I make the foolish mistake of marrying my lover?" Berni wondered.

Why does marriage turn sex into such a solemn act? Before, we made love without worrying about the bed or whether we had blankets. How things change. Did it matter, like it does now, to shower before and after?

Now, sex must be done in such a way that it no longer feels natural, as if it were a sin. Damn it, this is what makes marriages fail, Berni thought.

Indeed, these reflections were the very reasons that led to his separation from Maria Mercedes. She, too, treated sex like many wives do.

Berni didn't seem capable of living this new life. He accepted the changes happening in the world and in people's lives, but he didn't want it to affect his sexual life, and especially not his own, he thought as he headed to the airport. On his way back home, he picked up the mail left by the postal truck. Among the advertisements and false offers from merchants of the global world, he found a letter from his brother, dated two days earlier. Jaime was studying English in prison. His letter was filled with many words in the language of Americans— the language of business, of "Bussines." Jaime had realized that learning the language of the North Americans would open new opportunities for him when he was released, and, above all, help him avoid the abuse he had been suffering from the guards at the reform school.

Berni replied and congratulated him on his studies, assuring him that once people knew he could speak English, he would earn respect. He also wrote that Jaime should remember that the New World would not be governed by diplomatic, political, religious, or sexual relationships, but by economic ones. For this, the best thing was to know English. He wrote: "French is for diplomacy, Italian is for romance, English is for business, but above all, for speaking with God, no language is better than Spanish."

Berni knew the problems prisoners faced, not just in the United States, but in prisons around the world—overcrowding, abuse, drug addiction, misinformation, and, above all, injustice. He learned about this in his criminology studies at the University of Santiago. Berni

165

visited his brother and also received letters from other inmates, including some Cubans.

Berni waited for his wife to unpack. After his son went out to deliver a gift to one of his friends, he told his wife he was waiting for her to give her the accumulated affection. She, understanding what he meant, replied that she wasn't feeling well, but with a wink, confirmed, "I'm not feeling well, but I'll be back later."

Berni turned his thoughts to Colombia and began planning his next vacation.

Two weeks later, Berni was sitting at his brother Arge's house. He went straight to see him, without even stopping by the Juanchito nightclubs, because he knew his brother was seriously ill with cancer and was already showing the pain that victims of such diseases experience. He even had to go to the Social Security offices to advance the procedures for his pension, which he was entitled to after turning 60—an age that was fast approaching.

Unknowingly, this would be Berni's last visit to his brother, and it was very different from the others. There was no liquor, no women, and no discussions of their usual matters. They talked about business, finance, new clients, and strikes by transporters, which greatly affected Arge. They also discussed other matters regarding Buenaventura and the country. During the conversation, the topic of family and friends came up.

"Your country, my dear little brother, is heading toward the bottom of the abyss," Arge said. "Corruption runs from the presidency office all the way down to under that wooden bridge you see over there. The UPAC system has destroyed the middle class. The predominant religion is no longer Catholicism because Christians are proselytizing, and they're finding it easy to convert people because faith has been lost."

"How's that, brother?" Berni asked.

"Well, the Christians preach faith in Christ," Arge replied. "They are reconnecting people with the lost faith. The worst part is that the Catholic Church isn't doing anything to prevent it."

"Good, my dear, that's a good conclusion. The Catholic Church isn't doing its part because it doesn't want to deceive its people again. They, the pope and the cardinals, know that the matter of one church or another is a matter of gender, but not of substance. Remember, the Catholic pope is looking for reconciliation with the other churches in the world, and in the end, this or many future popes won't matter; the Church will be one. But that's something we'll have to wait for," said Arge.

"Speaking of this," Arge continued, "what do you think about my little fat son coming to perform an exorcism on me because he thinks I have the devil inside? He says he's going to baptize me and save my soul."

At that moment, Arge stood up. "I confess I can't bear it. I hope that soon you get the forgiveness you asked for from the President of the United States, and I'll receive it with open arms and throw a big party for you, like the prodigal son in the biblical passage." At that moment, tears began to fall from his eyes, but he couldn't continue. Berni stood up, embraced him, and kissed him on the cheek. He waited for him to cry as long as he needed. Later, Berni invited him to walk outside the house, and they went together down the path. Berni spoke to him about other matters, like the motorcycle parts business that was thriving in the city and Colombia. Arge told him he had been invited by the Japanese to visit their country, but because of his illness, he had to decline the invitation.

Nine months after this day, the man who could easily have been the one to love his son the most on earth passed away.

They talked for three continuous days without drinking a drop. During their conversations, they discussed the presidential elections, in which Dr. Horacio Serpa Uribe and Andrés Pastrana, among others, were running. Not because of a lack of honesty, but because they didn't belong to the political caste, they weren't sons of politicians, or simply because they belonged to outsider parties like communism.

"And speaking of elections, my dear brother," said Arge, "who are you thinking of voting for?"

"Well, brother, since you ask, I'll be voting for Dr. Horacio Serpa Uribe, not because he's my favorite saint or the savior of the country, but because I'll do it out of liberal discipline. Besides, the greatest and most wonderful thing about democracy is exactly voting for democracy, even if it's temporarily named Horacio, Andrés, Rousseau, Montesquieu, Thomas Jefferson, or John F. Kennedy."

"So, none of the main candidates inspire your trust?" asked Arge.

"That's right. They don't inspire anything. A good candidate is one who can show justice for the poor, and they don't measure up for that. They are the same as we've seen for a long time: gentlemen who, once elected, pass through the government without leaving a trace. Nothing at all, not even socialists of the caliber of Alfonso López Michelsen or Belisario Betancourt."

"But what about poverty in the United States? What happens there with such good and honest presidents?" asked Arge.

"Look, brother," said Berni, "in the United States, we also have poverty, and a lot of it, but the difference is that they have such well-organized and well-channeled social programs that people don't easily detect the poor. They're just as miserable as those here, but they line up to receive help behind walls, unlike governments like in Colombia, where the poor are kept on the streets. Another way to hide poverty is through capital loans. Workers are 'favored' with long-term money to buy a house, a car, or pay for education, but half of them don't manage to finish the payments, and the other half, when they finish paying the debt, have paid three times the amount they received, and the things, goods, or furniture they paid for are already worthless!"

"Can you give me an example of what you're talking about?" asked Arge.

"Sure," said Berni. "Let's say you take out a $50,000 loan over 30 years, and in the end, after 30 years, you'll have paid the bank $180,000, including interest and costs. The house you bought after 30 years will be falling apart because it's made with disposable materials. And everything you know could be lost in a hurricane, destroyed by a storm, or consumed by fire."

"That country is economically powerful because nobody escapes paying taxes, and they have a savage system of multiplying capital so it doubles every five years at least. The money that circulates the most is credit card money, and these have an average annual interest of 18%. Notice how they work with money. People leave their money with a 9% annual interest rate in a savings account, and the same entity grants them—without them asking—a credit card with 18% annual interest. Now, check this out: the computerized banking system gives the capital owner the advantage of turning one dollar into three, because of the speed of detection, that dollar is reinvested. In other words, in a cubicle in a bank office, you're signing the receipt of a loan, but that money stays in the bank, and in another branch, another customer is doing the same thing, and so on. This phenomenon is so impressive that we have people who take out a loan and don't withdraw the money; they only care about having the credit, which is in the end the letter of existence. If you're not in the credit regime, you don't exist. It's that simple. The worst part is that every day the poor are buying the most expensive poverty."

"The result of this phenomenon is that future generations will have to buy their own poverty. Many years ago, the poor were just poor, but with the global neoliberal system, now they have to pay dearly for their poverty."

At that moment, Beatriz, Arge's daughter, noticed her father with his mouth open. She took him by the arm and led him to the table, inviting the others present to eat.

The conversation continued on topics of general interest, and soon the obligatory question came up: "What do you know about Jaime, your brother? When is he getting out of prison?"

"My brother," Berni answered, "has to serve at least half of his sentence, meaning six years and one day. It's easy to know the day and hour someone enters prison, but no one knows the day and hour of release. He'll be deported to this country when he's free, and of course, they'll hand him over to the authorities here for processing. By the way, I'm receiving many letters from Cubans in prison who have served 2, 3, or 5 years of their sentences and are still there, just because Cuba—or rather, Fidel Castro—won't accept them. This is the most shameful crime of the U.S. government, and no one has spoken out to condemn this violation of human rights."

Berni felt happy to be with his family from Buenaventura, whom he had always loved, and strangely, neither he nor his brother drank a drop of liquor. He had profound respect for Arge's illness, the son of Doña Carmen, who had not become the Pope of the Catholics because of a stupid rumor from a woman who loved him without him knowing—the first platonic love that ever existed.

When Berni arrived in Cali, he went straight to the offices of Dr. Quijano, his former Criminal Law professor and dean of the University, to present the case of the pension Berni wanted to claim from the Social Security Institute of Cali. His professor, as Berni called him, accepted the full authorization to help Berni with the recognition and payment of the pension, which Berni was entitled to after working for more than 10 years under the laws of Social Security in Colombia. Berni had worked for the first time at the age of 10 as a shopkeeper at the Belalcazar bakery, while still in the fourth grade of elementary school. From the day he accepted the position offered by his teacher, he never stopped working, except for the logical school vacations and holidays granted by company regulations for each year worked continuously.

Berni was six months away from turning 60, the first requirement of the law. The second was having worked and contributed for 500 weeks to Social Security. Berni had 2,600 weeks worked and paid, meeting both requirements. With pride, Berni signed the power of attorney for his former professor.

Dr. Quijano was still the same man—kind, polite, and very professional. He still had that pleasant, interesting, anecdotal conversation style of great conversationalists—like poet Otto de Greiff, statesman Laureano Gómez, former president López Michelsen, and writer and journalist Dr. Paneso Robledo.

His professor told Berni, without having received the first dollar in fees, "If you want to get the degree of lawyer from the University and the professional card from the Judiciary Council, I'm willing to help you with all the necessary procedures to graduate with honors." Berni thanked him for the offer and, recalling what had happened 25 years earlier, added, "When I get the retirement pension from the U.S. Social Security, which will happen in two more years, I'll return. If you still maintain the offer, I won't hesitate to take the exams required to graduate as a lawyer." "That's great," Dr. Quijano said. "I would love to see you as a judge."

Berni said goodbye to the respectable group accompanying him, including Dr. Quijano's children. He left the restaurant and went in search of other friends. Berni wanted to reconnect with everyone he had met during his time in Cali, the Sultana of the Valley, the city that had given him the happiest moments of his life—people and events he would never forget. He didn't remember the bitter times; those he had buried in the gardens of Central Park in New York.

Berni visited all his relatives one by one and expressed his love and memories. It felt like a farewell, as if he would never be seen again, as if he needed to tell everyone how deeply he loved them. He had never shown these signs of affection before, especially not in the way he had with the woman by his side. But this time, it wasn't in search of sexual love, which had once made him feel alive—it had been the reason for his life.

After his two-week vacation, Berni returned to Miami, where his wife Lilian was waiting for him at the airport. They embraced and kissed in an eternal kiss, and Berni whispered in her ear what he had never said before: "I love you like I've never loved any woman, and I swear I'll never go anywhere without your company." Berni was so sincere that Lilian trembled with emotion. But, ever suspicious, she looked into his eyes and asked, "Were you unfaithful?"

"No, don't worry. I came back as pure as I left," he replied. Lilian, terrified to hear her husband say this, fell silent as they drove home. He then shocked her further by saying he was going to transfer all of his property to her name, double the life insurance, withdraw the bank deposit certificates to be deposited in her name, and, lastly, he added, "Tomorrow, we'll go to the lawyer's office to have the will I wrote during the flight approved and legalized." Berni's voice became grave, and he spoke with unsettling certainty. Lilian was so stunned that she couldn't say anything. She thought, without speaking it aloud, "This feels like something tragic."

Chapter 11
Double Betrayals

That same night, Berni called his son, whom he loved so much, to the table and said things to him he had never said before. The first topic was the economy. He explained why the United States—his people, as he called them—was the leading economic power in the world. Marcos, at 13 years old, understood everything, not only because he was smart but also because the schools in this country taught economic activities before the first lesson in ethics. Marcos was deeply interested in the topics, and the next day, they continued their discussion about social issues like education, health, work, and immigration. The religious topic took several days to cover, not because Marcos didn't understand, but because with so many churches, it wasn't easy for Berni to leave each one with the same God.

To finish, Berni recommended his son always study. "Study the gospels, no matter the mysterious things they contain. Study philosophy, literature, read everything you see or pick up. Read books on economics, politics, science, stories, history, and never leave one unfinished. Learn at least one poem, for in every poem, there's a woman. Love women, but don't try to understand them. Trust people, but try to get to know them so you're prepared when they try to betray you. If someone does you wrong or betrays you, don't take revenge or hate anyone. Forgive everyone equally and admire the wonderful things each person has. Love your neighbor, but distinguish them without discriminating."

"Soon you'll be out on the street alone because you won't need to walk hand-in-hand with us, but we believe this because of the faith in our teachings and example. So, we hope no one will surprise you with anything. You should defend yourself from proposals to use drugs. Keep your senses alert at all times so you can prevent problems in time. But if one day you fall into something delicate, count on your father and mother, but before we can help you, call on God, because I might fail you, but He never will."

Wisdom will give you the ability to recognize liars, refute them with education and respect, but when dealing with a fool, leave him or change the subject. Be honest with yourself and others and never do wrong to anyone or do things that seem wrong.

After these talks, Marcos became closer to his father, and Berni considered him in all his affairs and plans. They were seen sharing like two brothers, despite the 47-year age difference between them—the age Berni was when his son was born in the Capital of the World, the city that never sleeps.

Marcos proudly said at school that he had real parents. From then on, his academic progress was notable, and his sympathy was recognized. Soon, he was named Centurion and elected as a student member of the National Honor Society.

Marcos was grateful to his parents, and one day, he told them that he promised them a scholarship to save the money they had been paying for his prepaid university program. "No, son, thanks for your good intentions, but it's you who should promise or commit, not us," his mother, Lilian, said. Then they all kissed.

"The result of this phenomenon is that future generations will have to buy their own poverty. Many years ago, the poor were just poor, but with the global neoliberal system, now they have to pay dearly for their poverty."

At that moment, Beatriz, Arge's daughter, noticed her father's surprised expression. She took him by the arm and led him to the table, inviting the others present to eat.

The conversation continued with topics of general interest, and eventually, the obligatory question came up: "What do you know about Jaime, your brother? When is he getting out of prison?"

"My brother," Berni answered, "has to serve at least half of his sentence, which means six years and one day. It's easy to know when someone enters prison, but no one knows when they will be released. He will be deported to this country once he's free, of course, and handed over to the authorities here to be processed. By the way, I'm receiving many letters from Cubans in prison who have served 2, 3, or even 5 years of their sentence and are still there simply because Cuba—or rather, Fidel Castro—won't accept them. This is the most shameful crime of the U.S. government, and no one has spoken out to condemn this violation of human rights."

Berni felt happy to be with his family from Buenaventura, whom he had always loved. Strangely, neither he nor his brother drank a drop of liquor. He had profound respect for Arge's illness, the son of Doña Carmen, who hadn't become the Pope of the Catholics due to a foolish rumor from a woman who loved him without him knowing—the first platonic love that ever existed.

When Berni arrived in Cali, he went straight to the office of Dr. Quijano, his former Criminal Law professor and dean of the University, to present the case for the pension Berni wanted to claim from the Social Security Institute of Cali. His professor, as Berni called him, accepted the full authorization to help Berni with the recognition and payment of the pension, to which Berni was entitled after working for over 10 years. Berni had started working at the age of 10 as a shopkeeper at the Belalcazar bakery while still in the fourth grade of elementary school. From that moment, he never stopped working, except for school vacations and holidays granted by company regulations for each year worked continuously.

Berni was six months away from turning 60, the first requirement of the law. The second requirement was having worked and contributed for 500 weeks to Social Security. Berni had worked and paid for 2,600 weeks, meeting both criteria. With pride, Berni signed the power of attorney for his former professor.

Dr. Quijano was still the same man—kind, polite, very professional, and, above all, still possessing that pleasant, interesting, anecdotal conversation style of the great conversationalists—like poet Otto de Greiff, statesman Laureano Gómez, former president López Michelsen, and writer and journalist Dr. Paneso Robledo.

Without even receiving the first dollar in fees, his professor told Berni, "If you want to get the degree of lawyer from the University and the professional card from the Judiciary Council, I'm willing to help you with all the necessary procedures to graduate with honors." Berni thanked him for the offer and, recalling what had happened 25 years earlier, added, "When I get my retirement pension from the U.S. Social Security, which will happen in two years, I'll return. If you still maintain the offer, I won't hesitate to take the exams required to graduate as a lawyer."

"That's great," Dr. Quijano said, "I would love to see you as a judge."

Berni said goodbye to the respectable group accompanying him, including Dr. Quijano's children. He left the restaurant and went in search of other friends. Berni wanted to reconnect with everyone he had met during his time in Cali, the Sultana of the Valley—the city that had given him the happiest moments of his life. People and events he would never forget. He didn't dwell on the bitter times; those he had buried in the gardens of Central Park in New York.

Berni visited all his relatives one by one, expressing his love and sharing memories. It felt like a farewell, as if he would never be seen again, as if he needed to tell everyone how deeply he loved them. He had never shown these signs of affection before, especially not to the woman by his side. But this time, it wasn't about seeking sexual love—what once had made him feel alive—it was the reason for his life.

After the two-week vacation, Berni returned to Miami, where his wife Lilian was waiting for him at the airport. They embraced and kissed in an eternal kiss, and Berni whispered in her ear what he had never told her before: "I love you like I've never loved any woman, and I swear I'll never go anywhere without your company." Berni was so sincere that Lilian trembled with emotion. But, ever suspicious, she looked into his eyes and asked, "Were you unfaithful?"

"No, don't worry. I came back as pure as I left," he replied. Lilian, terrified to hear her husband say this, stayed silent as they drove home. He then shocked her further by telling her that he was going to transfer all his property to her name, double the life insurance, withdraw the bank deposit certificates so she could deposit them in her name, and added, "Tomorrow, we'll go to the lawyer's office to have the will I wrote during the flight approved and legalized." Berni's voice became grave, and he spoke with unsettling certainty. Lilian was so stunned that she couldn't respond. She thought, silently, "This feels like something tragic."

That same night, Berni called his son, whom he loved dearly, to the table and said things to him he had never said before. The first topic was the economy. He explained why the United States—his people, as he called them—was the leading economic power in the world. Marcos, being a 13-year-old teenager, understood everything, not only because he was smart but also because the schools in this country taught economic activities before the first lessons in ethics. Marcos was deeply interested in the topics, and the next day, they continued their discussion about social issues like education, health, work, and immigration. The religious topic took several days to discuss, not because Marcos didn't understand it, but because with so many churches, it wasn't easy for Berni to leave each one with the same God.

To finish, Berni recommended his son always study. "Study the gospels, no matter the mysterious things they contain. Study philosophy, literature, read everything you see or pick up. Read books on economics, politics, science, stories, history, and never leave one unfinished. Learn at least one poem, for in every poem, there's a woman. Love women, but don't try to understand them. Trust people, but try to get to know them so you're prepared when they try to betray you. If someone does you wrong or betrays you, don't take revenge or hate anyone. Forgive everyone equally and admire the wonderful things each person has. Love your neighbor, but distinguish them without discriminating."

"Soon you'll be out on the street alone because you won't need to walk hand-in-hand with us, but we believe this because of the faith in our teachings and example. So, we hope no one will surprise you with anything. You should defend yourself from proposals to use drugs. Keep your senses alert at all times so you can prevent problems in time. But if one day you fall into something delicate, count on your father and mother, but before we can help you, call on God, because I might fail you, but He never will."

177

Wisdom will give you the ability to recognize liars, refute them with education and respect, but when dealing with a fool, leave him or change the subject. Be honest with yourself and others and never do wrong to anyone or do things that seem wrong.

After these talks, Marcos became closer to his father, and Berni considered him in all his affairs and plans. They were seen sharing like two brothers, despite the 47-year age difference between them— the age Berni was when his son was born in the Capital of the World, the city that never sleeps.

Marcos proudly said at school that he had real parents. From then on, his academic progress was notable, and his sympathy was recognized. Soon, he was named Centurion and elected as a student member of the National Honor Society.

Marcos was grateful to his parents, and one day, he told them that he promised them a scholarship to save the money they had been paying for his prepaid university program. "No, son, thanks for your good intentions, but it's you who should promise or commit, not us," his mother, Lilian, said. Then they all kissed.

Berni had been doing things very well, almost perfectly. But it wasn't clear whether this change in attitude was due to the panic of his brother's terminal illness or simply an attempt to rectify and redirect his life. Either way, the transformation was evident, and his family and friends noticed it. Whenever the opportunity arose, he would express his love for people. At home, he was more sympathetic than ever. He spoke with people, exchanged ideas, taught what he knew, and sought out what he wanted to learn. He studied, read, wrote, and instead of going out on the streets searching for love from women, he sat at the computer and began writing a book—a story about what had happened and the circumstances surrounding it. He even dared to write about what hadn't happened. Fiction or not, he wanted it written down. It was, after all, the only thing left for him to do.

From Buenaventura came the news that finally, the Christians in Arge's house had agreed to let a Catholic priest administer the sacred anointing to their father and grandfather. This ceremony, according to Catholic beliefs, was given to anyone in danger of death. His son Gabriel entered proudly with Father Ruiz, a man distinguished by his faith and service to God, the church, and the community. He was also a friend of Arge. It's unknown what Arge confessed to Father Ruiz, but what is known is that less than 24 hours later, Arge passed away, just two hours after hearing of his father's death.

Incredible, Father Ruiz was never the same after that confession. No one will ever know what affected him so deeply, as neither of them spoke to anyone after the last rites until their deaths. Berni wasn't surprised by this; he knew his brother had been mentally ill when he found out he was going to die irreparably. He thought he knew half of his life, or so he believed.

During this time, Pastor Fernel, calling from the Texas prison, attempted to give Arge a spiritual baptism to save him from death. He hoped Arge would rise after the session and then go to the notary in Buenaventura to sign his will. The result of Pastor Fernel's failure was better for the Christian church. If he had saved his father by phone at that moment, humanity would have known about it in minutes, and no one would go to church seeking physical or spiritual salvation—this would be solved by phone or the internet. Save God the churches.

Berni was now looking inside himself, searching for logic in people—something that had never interested him before. He wanted to rectify. He was convinced that people shouldn't wait for others to change; one must change oneself. No one is here to assimilate another's lesson, especially now; everyone is living their own life. Mirrors don't reflect others' faces but your own. He understood that no one should be domesticated by someone else as if they were animals. Each person must be their own being, with their own experience.

As time passed in the United States, Berni wrote articles for the *Nuevo Herald* of Miami, covering topics such as economics, social programs, politics, religion, and sex. Among these, he published *The Elements of Temptation*, a direct allusion to the 1998 U.S. Presidential scandal, which stated:

"Temptation can be seen everywhere and at all times, especially at work, at school, at home, in the neighborhood, in churches, and when we travel. The most dangerous temptations are money, food, and sweets. Food takes the form of a woman or a man, and unfortunately, it also appears as a child. It attacks without distinction of race, sex, color, religion, or condition. It makes everyone fall equally, from simple people to the privileged—kings, presidents, popes, bishops, priests, pastors, nuns, seminarians, athletes, or artists. No one is safe."

The first victim, I still remember because it affected me with its stupidity, was a man named Adam. When he succumbed to temptation, disguised as a talking snake (since at that time snakes could speak), he blamed Eve, who couldn't respond because her body trembled. The consequences of this act were so severe that we are still paying for that mistake: we lost paradise, were forced to work, and then to die. How would today's world be if the laws enacted by legislators had copied divine law—the law to die for committing the sexual act, or for falling into sexual temptation? I write what I imagine: there would be no more than twelve people inhabiting the earth. As for me, I would have been sitting in the electric chair since my unforgettable fifteen years.

Few escape. King David (Jerusalem, 587 BC) faced the most terrible temptation. He committed a crime to satisfy it. The story says he sent Bathsheba's husband to the front lines of battle so that he would be killed by the enemy, and afterward, he slept with the temptation—he became ill when he saw Bathsheba bathing in front of the palace terrace. The result of his uncontrolled passion was the end of his reign.

The case of William Jefferson Clinton was very close to temptation. The man fell, not the President, because in that moment, he was no more than a simple mortal, and one can't think of the wife, children, family, society, government, or the state.

Be careful with the kids. Hundreds of thousands, perhaps millions, of young people, just discovering the world, fall victim to the temptation of sex and are forced to abandon their studies and university dreams, without even enjoying their adolescence, family, or friends. As parents, we must be very careful with our children because they are being pursued in schools; they are awaited outside or on their way home, like the unforgettable Jimmy Ryce. The worst part is that often, the temptation is inside the house itself, operating in just a few minutes, while parents return from the supermarket or work.

Berni also wrote about the Cuban exile in an article published in *Diario del Exilio* in the November 16, 1996 edition.

Marco Aurelio, the son of Doña Carmen, was ultimately the only Gomez to stay in Colombia. He loved his children so much that he couldn't move to the North. His trips could have ended in tragedy due to his absence. When his mother threw his father out on the street, his children declared a permanent hunger strike—without water—forcing their mother to bring their father back. Once they sat down at the table with their food, they considered the strike over. The eldest was only 10 years old. This proud man was in better conditions than any resident of the United States because he didn't have to pay what they call "mortgage"—a monster that, with its insatiable appetite, devours the money, skin, and brain of workers. Marco Aurelio was the owner of the house where he lived with his family. He was the only son of Doña Carmen who, without being foolish, saw the virgin. His sister Lucila, the best daughter that ever existed, gave it to him one day—not even his birthday. He, as a member of the intelligent group, never rented, mortgaged, or sold it, always keeping it for the well-being of his children, grandchildren, and descendants.

In New Jersey, **Luzmila**, the little blonde with blue eyes from Doña Carmen, would remain forever. She never married again or joined any man, and much less served sex on demand. It's unknown how she managed to live the rest of her life, but she never used the "orgasmotron" method—a system, by the beginning of the new century, that would be sold to make women reach orgasm without relations with a man. This asexual, despicable invention was rejected by Luzmila, the disillusioned, and, as it appeared one day, it disappeared as well. Her health was cared for by doctors, and with their wisdom, they kept her alive without saving her life. Finally, on a hot day in September 2002, Luzmila, mother of Hernán, passed

181

away at her house in New Jersey. The doctors ensured she passed without suffering, though she desperately clung to life until the very end.

Jaime, the one who urinated in bed until his mother, Doña Carmen, threatened to tell a young woman interested in him, was on the prison list. He was the most dangerous of all, not only for his long tongue, which was noticeable as soon as he spoke, but for his actions and omissions. Without having killed a fly, he caused great harm to his family and those around him. He was the only one of the eleven children who ended up in prison. If Don Marco had still been alive, his son would have had no choice but to remain in prison. And if Doña Carmen had still been alive, she would have spent six years crying, for her river of tears never dried, despite the attacks against her.

Even behind bars, Jaime caused immense economic harm to U.S. taxpayers. He was the most expensive prisoner of all. Due to his hemophilia, he was frequently admitted to the hospital. Halfway through his sentence, he had already undergone multiple surgeries, including one for a hernia in his genital area that he'd suffered from since his youth. Doctors performed the surgery knowing his medical condition, though it was unclear if they did so out of necessity or to take advantage of taxpayer contributions. The son of Doña Carmen died for a time, for just over 10 days, but came back to life after six months. He was saved by advances in medicine, absorbing factor 8 as a coagulant, and because the Crucified Lord heard his pleas to save him. If he had asked the Lord to save his soul, he would have died irreparably. Jaime remains the most devout believer in Jesus Christ, unlike his mother, who was the number one devotee of the Sacred Heart of Jesus.

Berni's old age was in danger.

Foreseeing all these challenges, 14 years ago, Berni went to the U.S. Social Security office and demanded they recognize the contributions he had made using a fictitious number. In reality, Berni had contributed from 1984 to 1987, but Social Security only acknowledged payments starting in 1988, when he acquired his residence and personal Social Security number. Berni didn't think it was right, especially coming from such a respectable government like the U.S. government. So, dressed in a suit and tie, he sat confidently and, with crossed legs and in fluent English, said the same words he had been practicing for two months:

"My dear and respected sir, I am here to request that you recognize my right to obtain the accumulated amount of my contributions, starting from the very first payment made in my name. This money was sent by my employer in my name, and since I am the same person, and you never returned those sums despite knowing where to find me, I can't believe such a serious and responsible entity like this would try to keep money that doesn't belong to them. If someone sent me money that wasn't mine, I would return it immediately. Of course, you will return it to me upon my retirement, but I hope that while this happens, these sums are reflected in my records and to my benefit. I expect a response soon, because from now on, I will not sleep with the same peace of mind as before. Please convey my respects to him and tell him I await a favorable response."

More than a year passed before Social Security finally recognized Berni's contributions. When he received the news, he cried, reflecting on the millions of dollars that the Mexican Social Security for the elderly had, which they had never returned.

Berni decided to travel to Cali to receive his payment, but after so many telephone calls from Miami with his lawyer's secretary at the Social Security office, he wasn't sure if he wanted to receive the money or simply wanted to see the charming and friendly Bety La Bella again. It turned out to be the latter. She was there, waiting for him at the exit for international passengers at Bonilla Aragón Airport in Cali. Berni was struck by how much more beautiful she was in person than the photo he had received through the internet, which he had kept in his coat pocket before leaving Miami. She didn't have the measurements of a queen, but she had everything for a king, and Berni was the right man to make her feel royal.

After greeting each other with a hug (Berni avoided a kiss, needing to be sure she hadn't been followed by a man), they exchanged pleasantries. In the car Berni had rented for his time in the "Capital of Joy," Bety offered to take him to explore the city.

"Well," Berni clarified, "remember, I lived here for most of my life, dear Bety. I know exactly what you told me on the phone, but I must tell you, Cali is a very different city now."

She sat next to Berni in the front seat as they drove, and Berni looked back at the cars following them. Without her realizing, he took a turn at the roundabout and headed north. When he checked again, none of the cars that had been following them were behind. Later, Bety realized the direction Berni was heading and pointed it out.

"You're lost, Berni. This is not the way to the city center," she said.

Berni placed his finger on his lips and said, "Yes, it's true, I'm lost, but how wonderful it is to be lost with a woman like you. And it would be even more beautiful if no one found us."

Berni knew exactly where he was going. The car was headed toward the outskirts of the city, toward Yumbo, the industrial capital of Valle del Cauca, a place 20 minutes away where Berni had spent very special moments. As the sun set over the valley, the skies turned golden, forming strange shapes. The heat of the day dissipated as Berni's body adjusted to the cool of the evening. He remembered an article he had written for his Miami newspaper column, *The Elements of Temptation*, and mentally apologized to former President Bill Clinton for his escapades in the White House.

The next day, Berni went back to his lawyer's office, collected the investment certificates he had left in a financial institution, and paid for the legal services. He kissed the secretary on the cheek in front of her boss, thanking her for her help.

The address where Berni had gone the previous night was given to Bety, as requested by Berni when he was in Miami, though she didn't know the details. She never asked, as she was discreet.

On his way to the house of the woman who had received such a beautiful serenade, Berni thought about how he would tell her that

184

he still loved her, that he had never forgotten her, and that he would always speak to the moon, asking if it knew how she was and whether she was happy. But she was married. Shortly after Berni had married his pregnant lover, she had given herself to another man in a Catholic ceremony. It would be very difficult for Berni to arrange a meeting with her. There were many factors that made any infidelity from her side impossible: her husband was a man of virtues Berni lacked—faithful, unlike most Colombians. He had loved her from the first day they met, and his love had only grown over time. He was a true man, husband, and father. Berni knew this not because they had treated him well, but because he had hired a private investigator who had uncovered everything. Berni waited for an opportunity to offer support to Esmeralda, but that moment never came. Her husband never mistreated her, nor was there any reason for her to leave or separate. He didn't drink, smoke, or use drugs, and he wasn't a vagabond. Berni also knew she wasn't in town.

The previous night, Berni had arrived at her house and, being cautious, didn't cause any trouble. He made several rounds around the block, observing, but couldn't see her. He didn't knock on the door, unsure if she would open it.

Realizing it was time to go to the airport and return to Miami, Berni dropped off the rented car and headed to the American Airlines counter. At the airport, his wife Lilian and son Marco Antonio were waiting for him.

Back home, Berni sat at the computer and ordered an Internet subscription to keep up with Cali's social news and the life of the city that had once kept his happiness at bay. Every day, since his arrival, he opened the pages of *El País* and was updated via email by his private agent on the couple's movements.

Berni's life was now completely content. His wife loved him deeply, and his children, Marco Antonio and the two from his previous marriage to Maria, visited him often, along with his grandchildren. At work, he had earned the trust of his superiors due to his honesty and reliability and had one of the best salaries in the company. The workweek was ideal—Monday to Friday—giving Berni the flexibility that most people in Miami, a tourist city, desired.

Berni's economic future was secure, thanks to his salary, U.S. Social Security retirement pension, and investments in Colombia. The latter was secured in case of firm bankruptcy, which would cover all his expenses if he decided to live in Cali. His youngest son's university fees were already paid for, and Marco Antonio's medical school fees were saved for four years in advance. Everything was covered, except for the beautiful house they owned in Miami's luxury Kendall area. In case of emergency, Berni had a deposit to cover three months of mortgage payments, along with a life insurance policy in the bank's safety deposit box, all in Lilian's name, except for the time deposits in Colombia, which were in Berni's name.

As for his physical health, Berni was in excellent condition, with no signs of illness. His doctor, who checked on him every six months, congratulated him for his well-being. Products like Viagra, hormones, vitamins, or any kind of natural supplements from China or Japan had no place in Berni's life. He had no need for them. Since his youth, when adult magazines and porn videos began to enter Colombia, he was one of the first to access them as an employee at an insurance company. However, he never paid attention to them. He loved nudity and the beauty of women but had been traumatized after watching a film depicting a woman and a dog. He never again watched adult content, and to this day, when he saw a woman with a dog, it made him uneasy. He would jokingly say, "Sorry to the women who love their dogs so much," but people didn't understand him.

Not everyone understood Berni, and neither did Esmeralda, the woman who received his serenade. For days afterward, she wondered about the identity of the romantic serenader who had remained a mystery, hidden in the shadows. Berni knew in advance that her husband would return the next day and that he wouldn't cause her any trouble.

"Nothing, well, pay attention," Berni said, a calm tone to his voice. "Ten minutes before visiting hours end, I'll go to the bathroom. You wait outside. When I knock from the inside, you enter, remove your clothes, including your underwear. I'll put on your uniform, and you'll wear my clothes. Put on these contact lenses—green, like my eyes. I'll wear these brown ones like yours. Then, we leave together, sit here. When I give the signal to leave, you'll follow behind the others. At the last door, there are two guards. You'll show them the card you're wearing and they'll return your driver's license. Walk slowly to the blue Camry, parked on the right. Inside, you'll find a cap like mine. There's a suitcase with clothes for you in the trunk. You'll change once we hit the interstate. The car's full of gas, and there's money in the suitcase. Car documents are in the glove compartment. You can go wherever you want, but remember, your name is Berni. Don't show up at my house saying 'here I am,' because my wife will recognize you. She doesn't like these things."

He paused for a moment, then continued: "Has anything changed in the meal distribution system or routines? Any new developments? I'm staying in bed for three days, and I'll speak little to avoid any questions I can't answer."

Berni waited for Jaime's reply and then said, "Do not take off the lenses for any reason. If they bother you, use one of those liquids they sell everywhere. I'll wet them with my tears, knowing you're free. Take care, my brother. Look for the key in my compartment under the bed's north side leg. Don't forget it."

When Berni stood up, he realized the inmates' bathroom was not the same as the visitors' bathroom. He instructed Jaime to knock on the door when he was ready. Two minutes later, Jaime did so, and within moments, both brothers exited and sat at the same table. By the time the visit ended, over half the seats were empty. The lines for the goodbyes were long, and most people were hugging and crying.

Berni whispered to Jaime, "No one noticed a thing. Look at how distracted the guards are."

Jaime was starting to feel nervous, but Berni reassured him. As they stood and embraced, Berni said loudly, "See you soon, Berni. Don't forget to come back."

Jaime understood the cue and responded, "I'll be back next week. Don't forget to take care of that cold, dear Jaime."

Chapter 12
Legacy

The brothers, though not born at the same time, were twins in every way—identical in appearance, mannerisms, and voice. Their resemblance was so striking that even the guard didn't stop to check Berni when he was registered for the return to the cell. Berni headed straight for the library to hide for a while.

Meanwhile, Jaime moved through the next checkpoints. The guard at the last door looked at him, but when Jaime opened his eyes, the green contact lenses were visible. The guard casually remarked, "Are you living in Miami? Beautiful city."

Jaime simply nodded. The guard handed him his driver's license and directed him toward the exit. As Jaime walked through the gate to freedom, he felt his legs shake, and when he reached the car, he sat in the driver's seat, staring at the sky. The vast beauty of the world overwhelmed him. He felt a deep connection to the universe—at peace with himself for the first time in ages.

While looking in the rearview mirror, he caught a glimpse of Dona Carmen's resemblance. Overcome by emotion, a contact lens slipped from his eye and hung from his cheek. As he wiped away the tears, a guard approached and knocked on the window. "Okay, okay," Jaime muttered, quickly starting the car and driving away.

He headed south toward Miami, the road ahead feeling symbolic of his own journey. The path to freedom had started, and Jaime thought about life—how beautiful it could be, and how difficult it was to truly live it.

As he neared a sign for the city of Ola, Jaime turned off the road, intending to visit his sisters, Miryam and Lilia. After stopping at a service station, he called Miryam, who answered after two rings. Jaime requested her address, then drove to her house.

When Miryam opened the door, she hugged him tightly, amazed at the sight of her brother. "But Bernito, why didn't you tell me you were coming?" she exclaimed.

"I'm that fool you're referring to. I'm Jaime," he replied.

"Jaime? No way! But yes, my God, it's really you." Miryam was in shock, hugging him again. She couldn't believe it.

They spoke for a while, with Jaime telling his sister about his time in prison, but his focus quickly shifted to finding Lilia. "Where's Lilia?" he asked.

"She'll be here soon. She's just at the store. Come, sit down. I'll make something to eat," Miryam offered.

"No, thank you, sister. I just came to greet you. I'm heading to Miami to see my daughters," he said, before getting back into the car and heading to the interstate.

As Jaime drove, he couldn't help but reflect on the importance of family. At 7:30 p.m., he arrived in front of his daughter Gloria's house. He was overwhelmed with emotion. Without waiting, he rushed out of the car, shouting for her. The shock and confusion on her face were clear, as her children ran in every direction and her husband stood frozen.

Later, in the living room, Gloria's husband chuckled. "I thought you were going crazy, calling out for your daughter. But now, it's time for you to talk and tell us everything. How and why didn't they deport you?"

Jaime smiled and, after a moment of silence, lied about his situation. Gloria, hearing his story, left the room to prepare coffee.

With a soft chuckle, Jaime said, "Well, now that Gloria's here, I want to tell you I was granted conditional release," he paused, taking a deep breath, "thanks to a signed petition from Berni. I need to report back to the prison next Saturday for the final review, then I'll be free to go."

The tears came easily after that. Overcome with emotion, Jaime cried as his daughter comforted him. The glasses he was wearing slipped from his face, and he was caught in the moment.

"Why do you have green glasses, dad?" Gloria asked.

"Where are they?" Jaime fumbled. "I don't know how to handle these things." She cleaned the lenses and returned them to him.

"Those glasses were a gift from my brother Berni. I wore them so I could look like him and get a girlfriend easier."

Everyone laughed except for Jaime, who sat quietly, reflecting on his journey.

Jaime, known as "Tear" in Colombia for his emotional nature, had cried for 15 minutes and spent five minutes talking about his time in prison. But in that moment, he swore to himself he would never chase after problems again, whether related to drugs, alcohol, fights, or women.

"Stop, stop! What do you mean you won't go after women?" his daughter joked. "Is it true people come out of prison gay?"

Jaime replied, "Don't be an idiot. I won't chase after someone else's wife."

Jaime, ever the emotional man, had tried to blend back into normal life, but his temporary freedom came with complications. Berni, who had been through a similar experience, understood how difficult it was to step back into a life that hadn't been his for so long.

"Papa," said the youngest daughter, "we want to throw a party so everyone can come to the house and greet you."

"That's fine, daughter," Jaime replied, but he had something else on his mind. "This week, I'll be praying to God, thanking Him for His mercy."

His daughter, sensing his unease, said, "Mom will give you some money for any expenses, and with Gloria, we'll go shopping for some clothes for you." She paused. "By the way, where's your suitcase? How did you bring your clothes?"

"I left some books and letters for when I return," Jaime answered. "The rest, I gave away to my roommates."

"I'd like to drink some aguardiente," Jaime said, trying to lighten the mood. "I'm still very nervous."

"No problem," his daughter said and fetched a bottle from the bar. After drinking a few rounds, Jaime's voice became hoarse, but his spirits lifted, and he soon found himself dancing, joking, and re-immersed in the carefree atmosphere he once knew.

The party continued into the night, with visitors arriving and the festivities growing louder. Around midnight, Jaime slipped away unnoticed, heading off with a woman he'd just met. His sisters and the rest of the family thought little of it, as they were accustomed to Jaime's unpredictable behavior.

Three days passed with no word from Jaime. The family, knowing Jaime's history and his tendency to disappear, refrained from contacting the authorities. Meanwhile, Berni, now in prison, faced the consequences of their earlier actions.

Final Chapter
30 Years, my Love

In prison, things had taken a turn for the worse. Berni's cover was blown, and his identity as Jaime was discovered by his cellmate, Bertulfo. The realization came when Bertulfo noticed a distinctive mole on Berni's foot that didn't match Jaime's. Bertulfo, though initially shocked, kept his suspicions to himself, allowing Berni time to think of a way out.

Berni knew his time was limited. He'd planned for his release, and Bertulfo, a fellow inmate from Cuba, was now part of that plan. "I'll be out this Saturday," Berni promised. "When I do, I'll help you get out. But I need information—your family's addresses. I need their signatures for the clemency petition."

Bertulfo, though initially hesitant, agreed to keep quiet and help Berni in return for his eventual freedom. "You're not Jaime," Bertulfo confirmed, but added, "Don't worry, I'll help you. Just keep your word."

By the end of the week, Berni's cold had passed, but the psychological toll of being discovered had a lasting effect. As he and Bertulfo discussed their plan in secrecy, Berni's mind raced, and he stayed alert, ready for the escape that was now only days away.

They spent the whole day together, and Bertulfo insisted that he was in prison because he hadn't paid the money owed to the owner of a speedboat who had brought part of his family to Miami.

"But how could the authorities convict you for a debt?" Berni asked.

"No, it wasn't that. What happened is that I got angry and started hitting the man because he treated me badly, and he called the police. Instead of telling the truth, he reported that I had broken into his house to rob him."

"Ah, I understand now. So the charges were based on the confession of the human trafficker, which ultimately brought you here."

"Exactly," Bertulfo said, getting up to go to the bathroom.

Berni was amazed by the story and thought about changing the conversation to try other methods to get to the truth.

"Anyway," he thought, "the alibi is well-constructed, but the prosecutors in this country don't believe anything. And when they use a jury, it's even worse because those people have no conscience. And if any of them turn out to be conscientious, the judge ensures they are removed from the case. When will they end this farce?"

That night, Bertulfo handed Berni the information about his family. "Trust me," he said while handing over the written paper. "Mariana will stay in bed reading a book I'll pick up from the library. If you notice any unusual movement, please come and let me know. When it's time for roll call, I'll be with you."

"Alright, Jaime," Berni replied, smiling. He leaned in closer to his ear and added, "If I find out you don't help me get out, I'm going to violate your dear little brother."

"Why is it that you Cubans are always thinking about that kind of thing?" Bertulfo laughed, and both men shared a hearty laugh.

The next morning, Berni walked slowly toward the prison chapel, where some people went to pray, others to cry, some to masturbate, and others to engage in sex in any form.

Berni soon prayed to God, asking for intervention for his brother, Jaime, to return. He passed by the library and took a book, *"Catch Me, Kill Me."* Berni read, but he didn't understand; it was just a way to minimize the fear running through his body and clouding his mind. He didn't hear anything—the prisoners passed by and shouted, "Since when has this crazy woman become a reader?"

Berni, terrified, couldn't stand up.

The causes converged to have an effect on him: fear on one side, dehydration from the fever on the other, the lack of faith in his brother and in God. Just three hours ago, he had confessed to the heart of Jesus that he was waiting confidently for Jaime's return.

In the seven days, he had lost seven pounds, which greatly worried him. He was also completely emaciated. The way out would be much more difficult compared to Jaime's presence and face. He could also be noticed during the entry check-in the visiting room, as only one hour would pass. "My God, divert the guards' gaze at that moment, or show me strong and healthy in their eyes."

Fifteen minutes before 2 p.m., Berni got up with great effort and began walking slowly in the dormitory, trying to steady himself on the floor. He was alert for the call. Thirty minutes passed after 2 p.m., and no one came to get him.

"I have to pray." He knelt by the bed, and at that moment, they called his name. "Gomez Restrepo, Jaime," the voice echoed throughout the place.

There was no one in the line, and the guard, after checking him from head to toe, said, "Leave that paper in the basket," pointing to the place. The man spoke to him in English. Berni crumpled the paper and threw it away to avoid walking. All the information about Bertulfo's family went into that basket.

Berni appeared in the room, radiant with happiness, and froze when he saw his brother. He was hanging from his shirt, and his pants were hanging from something unseen. They had no strength to stay on their feet and sat down. There were only 10 minutes left to finish the visit.

"What happened to you, little brother? Why are you in that state?" Jaime asked.

"That's what I want to know," replied Berni.

"Let's go to the bathroom. They're about to close it," said Jaime, and they got up. Jaime appeared at the door in the prisoner's uniform, and Berni in his brother's clean but wrinkled clothes.

In five minutes, Jaime told him that since he left until this morning, he had been rolling around in bed with a woman, not eating. "We only got up to sleep together. I think we drank water three or four times and took four or five bottles of aguardiente. I think I've not only lost seven pounds, but I've lost track of time. It's thanks to her that I'm here in front of you."

"My God, how great and merciful You are. Blessed be Your name."

He stood up, took a few steps back, and asked his brother for the car key. He handed it to him, and at that moment, Berni said, "Your keys are under the bed, in the same place where I found them. Goodbye, little brother, and may the Lord have mercy on you."

Berni left. The only difference with Jaime was the cap with the name "Miami" on the front.

"Take care, man, you look like you have AIDS," said Jaime, the new guard, who was working his first day at the prison.

Half an hour later, a Toyota car was gliding down Interstate 75 south, heading toward the Sun Capital. It was 3:30 p.m. on a Saturday. Berni swerved the car from side to side and sang along with Ana Gabriel's song *"Hasta llegar al mar."*

Berni arrived in Miami. Despite being in poor health, he drove so fast that when he overtook a Colombian without realizing it, the Colombian told his companions that "Montoya fever—the Formula One driver—has started."

But the fever was what drove him to his house. His wife greeted him, saying:

"Do you think it's nice to leave us alone for a week and then show up like this? Look at you, you look like a dollar-store Christ. What excuse do you have? Your son and I were calling your sisters' house, and they didn't know anything about you. Are you telling me you were in Ocala? You look more like you've been rolling around in bed with some prostitute or tramp."

Berni didn't respond and went in search of his bed. Several weeks passed before Lilian believed her husband's version about Jaime's escape.

But the guest from Hamilton Prison had already been in Colombia since the following Monday after his return, that is, the day after Sunday. He was taken at midnight to a vehicle that drove him to Miami, and from there, he flew to Bogotá and then to Cali. He was deported, and only after 20 years could he return to the United States. Behind him were his three beloved daughters, his wife, his brothers, including Berni, who gave him one of the most unforgettable weeks of freedom he had ever had.

It was after being in Cali that he understood the mistake he had made by acting as a mule for drug trafficking. He was 67 years old. No one hired him to work, he had no money to drink, and the worst part of the situation was that no woman paid him any attention. Tormented by sexual desire, he tried to seduce an older woman and failed. All the women seemed to agree, each letting him know, in their own way, that the global market didn't consider age, only capital.

But little brother, Jaime told Berni over the phone in a collect call to thank him for his help:

"It's incredible, just a few weeks ago in Miami, I was able to make love with a woman, and she paid for everything. A miracle, brother, a miracle."

Berni knew what he wanted and who he loved. When he received the first check from the U.S. Social Security pension, or rather, when he saw the amount deposited into his checking account, he thought he could now go live in Cali, the city that had once kept the woman he truly loved—Esmeralda.

Lilian was authorized to withdraw the necessary funds from the bank to live with her son, the best son in the world. As for Berni, he could

196

cover his expenses, including those of Esmeralda and her children when she separated from her husband. He never stopped thinking about this, and that's how it worked. He had planned everything.

"It's time," Berni said one night as he sat at his computer, reading the news from his beloved town of Colombia, the land with the smell of coffee and roses. "I have to leave. The strength of love pulls me. At least I'll live close to her. I'll choose a place where I can see her and wait for the opportunity to show her my love for the years I have left."

He quit his job and asked his wife to pack. But he told Lilian he had to leave immediately for Cali because the money he had left in the deposit was in danger of being lost, according to a newspaper article announcing the merger of the bank due to a loss of capital. This was a lie.

Two days later, Berni stood in front of the house of the love of his life.

He observed the movements around the house—who was coming and going, at what time. He watched his rival's car parked outside. He took note of how many children they had and their ages. The investigator frequently reported this information to Berni, but he was looking for only one thing, a five-letter word that never appeared in the reports. He wanted to know who was taking the children to school. "I hope they have a maid, and if I have to fall in love with her to get information, I will," he told himself.

Berni knew perfectly well that her husband had never been unfaithful, mistreated, or abused her, and this kept him from getting close to her. That's why Berni hadn't approached her before. Many times, he had sought out the husband under the pretext of discussing investments or interests in deposits in Colombia. Berni had made some investments with his guidance and help.

No one knew, especially not him, that Berni was only approaching him to learn more about her. Once, Berni asked how she was, and he answered, "She's fine." "Has she been sick?" Berni asked. "No, no," said Merardo, "there are better ones."

Berni felt like strangling him or throwing him to the floor with a slap, but with extraordinary effort, he controlled himself and changed the conversation. When he said goodbye, Berni left thinking about why the Virgin only appears to fools.

Berni was eager to see her again, face to face, and tell her that he loved her now more intensely than he did 30 years ago.

She left with one of her daughters and took her to the university. Then she drove her car to the city center. Berni followed at a cautious distance and entered a parking lot. He parked and, as he got out, hid behind a pair of Ray-Ban sunglasses and a cap. He took the elevator with her and got off one floor above her. After Esmeralda exited, he ran down the stairs, looking in every direction, but couldn't find her.

He waited again at the elevator door, pretending to read the tenant board. When she took the elevator down, Berni went to the office she had just exited and asked for her. The secretary replied that Mrs. Esmeralda had just left a few minutes ago, "But you can catch her in the elevator."

"Alright," Berni replied. "Please let me wait for her to return," and he sat down.

"No, sir. Why waste your time? She'll return next Friday to pick up the check."

"A check?" Berni asked. "But she told me you weren't going to pay her."

"Of course, we will pay her. The life insurance checks just take a while because they come from Bogotá."

"Oh, yes, yes. I understand now. So I'll return with her that day. What day did you say?"

"Friday," the secretary answered. "By the way, let me introduce myself. I'm B@mi Gomez, and your name?" he asked.

"My name is Milagros."

"Wonderful, I needed a person with such a beautiful name because I'm going to need miracles for real."

"Well, now you know. I'm at your service."

"Thank you, ma'am. You're very kind. See you soon."

Once outside, Berni noted the office number, which belonged to an insurance company he didn't know by name. The next day, Berni returned to the insurance company with a box of chocolates for Milagros. She received them gratefully, and Berni took the opportunity to ask her some questions, including what kind of insurance would be paid to Esmeralda. "She is the beneficiary of her husband's life insurance."

"Did he die?" — this was the word Berni always sought in the private agent's reports, in the news, in the newspapers, on the internet, asking people who called from Cali, or recommending to check with those going to Cali. He was a slave to this verb.

Absolutely no one suspected that Berni was patiently waiting for Merardo's death. Not even Merardo. How many times did Berni go to Colombia, asking personally or through others, but he was always following his steps? Once, he was talking with an eloquent friend, and this friend assured him that the only one who died to give eternal life was Jesus Christ.

"Excuse me, my dear, but I have another friend apart from the Savior, who with his death gives life."

"And who is that?" asked the believer.

"You'll know in due time," Berni answered.

A long time ago, when Berni and Esmeralda began seeing each other, she told him that there was a man in the company who was madly in love with her — it's unclear if she said this naively or to provoke jealousy. Berni responded, "I also die for you, but I'll wait until that man dies first."

This fateful phrase haunted him as a punishment to this day. Berni left almost running and barely raised his hand in a farewell gesture. Without waiting for the elevator, he ran down the stairs, managed to get outside, and continued running for more than 10 blocks until he was exhausted. He didn't care; or rather, he didn't think about the suspicious stares from people or the possibility of a police chase. He didn't know where he started drinking aguardiente, but contrary to what he always did—looking for a woman to go on a spree—he only limited himself to drinking.

"Dead man, beloved, to whom I offer all my respects," he said to himself, drunk.

He was lost in the liquor but knew he had to find himself on the most important Friday of his life. He woke up early, bathed as if he were getting married, dressed up, and stood in front of the main door of the building where the insurance company was located. Berni saw Esmeralda enter and followed her. He entered with her, but without showing his face. According to the secretary, she introduced him to Esmeralda as a client. Esmeralda froze, and staring into his eyes, she fainted. Thanks to Berni's attentiveness, he caught her in his arms before she hit the floor.

His heart was pounding hard, and it seemed like it was about to burst from his beautiful chest, which looked even more beautiful than before. She recovered slowly but maintained her dignified demeanor.

"But are you the Berni I knew in my youth?" she asked.

"Yes, I think it's you, because you still have those green eyes I'll never forget."

Berni didn't say a word, but he could have told her not to speak until he brought her a glass of sweetened water. He returned and asked her to drink the water. Then he told her he would take her to the doctor for an exam.

"No, thank you, Berni. I'm fine, believe me," she replied.

The secretary, scared but intelligent, took advantage of the situation to tell Esmeralda that her check hadn't arrived yet and that she should come back next Friday or earlier.

Berni overheard and thought that this gave him invaluable time, agreeing with the reason and saying, "Money is welcome any day."

When they left, Berni invited her to have coffee. She was still shaking. They sat down, and shortly after, an employee of the establishment attended to them. As they received their order, Berni said, "I'm so sorry about the passing of your husband. From now on, I'm ready to help you with anything you need. Believe me, I offer my cooperation from the heart."

"I don't know if I'll have another chance, but I must tell you something else. I love you more than before. I've never forgotten you, and the worst part is that I have no intention of forgetting you. You were, are, and always will be my only love. I've always had you in my heart and my thoughts, and only God knows how much I miss you."

"Berni, please. I never imagined that you still loved me," she said.

"You don't know how much I cried for you," she added.

Berni took her hands. "Destiny places people in different situations," he said. "This makes our paths deviate. In many cases, we are forced to leave the ones we love behind. How can I explain what happened? I still can't explain it myself. I have no life without you. You are the light, the hope. I've been living dead without you."

"Forgive me, but no matter what you say, I'm not going to separate from you. I've asked the moon every day about you, and I always beg her to take care of you. The stars know my anguish. When the wind passed by, I yelled at it to caress your skin for me, while I could. I always knew you were happy, and that comforted me when I became nostalgic. The stars gave me your reasons at night. My love, I offer you the purest feelings anyone could have."

201

"I can offer you unconditional support, and all I ask is that you allow me to be close to you—at least to see you and thank life for giving me everything, believing it would make me happy."

"How is it possible that you still love me, Berni? How much time has passed? Now I'm a widow. A whole life has passed, and now I belong to my children. I have five. Last Sunday, exactly one month after Merardo's passing"—Berni noted that she referred to his rival only by name—"I promised my children that I would dedicate myself exclusively to them. I won't fix my eyes on another man, and I won't marry again. I'll spend the rest of my years protecting them, taking care of them, and helping them with things like education and work. I'm sorry, Berni. It's too late."

"No, Esmeralda. I know it's too soon for you to talk about this. What I'm asking of you is simply to let me be your friend, to be attentive to your needs, and to help you with anything, if you need it. Don't feel obligated to me, nor break the promise you made to him," Berni thought while speaking.

Time was the best tailor to adjust or change the dress of women, and now Esmeralda wore the dress of both mother and father, in addition to the weight of widowhood. For now, she would wear her mother's style, Donia Carmen's, to take care of herself—another widow with dignity, like so many in the world, without moral or economic support.

"For every minute you allow me to be close to you, I will live one more year," Berni added.

"That's not true," Esmeralda replied. "I know you, I know your ways, and I know you're the same as always. Just yesterday, I heard you were with a very beautiful woman. I know it won't be enough for you just to see me."

Esmeralda added, "We must be realistic. We can't live our love like this."

Berni reached for her hands again, and when he felt their coldness, he understood that she was suffering and, evidently, that she still loved him.

"Our love," she said.

The expression left Berni more at ease. She turned pale and began to sweat. But he did not intend to make her suffer.

Serve me a brandy with milk and a coffee, he asked the employee who was passing near the table.

The encounter with Berni caused her great surprise. The love between the two could not be enjoyed despite having been very intense. She never thought that Berni could fall in love with her and she accepted it that way. She was confused now. Berni let her relax and to do so he changed the conversation. He said: "I have been observing the city and it is very transformed, beautiful and modern. I am delighted to be here, to see its people again, the progress and all."

Berni spoke to her for more than two hours. Her hands began to regain warmth and her face looked better. Berni contemplated her the way one contemplates sublime things. With love, with faith. Berni adored her. At this moment the most beautiful love story of a couple that destiny had separated could begin. She came out of her ecstasy and said to Berni, "I have to leave now."

"I feel like a stranger, as if I had not been on this planet. Forgive me for not giving you my phone number, another time I will let you know. And how can we see each other again?" asked Berni. "Next Friday I will be at the insurance office." She stood up and Berni pulled out the chair to give her space. She looked into his eyes and said again, "They are the same eyes I used to look into." She approached and kissed him on the cheek. Berni held her back and managed to kiss her lips softly. But for Berni it was enough; he had waited 30 years which for him were 100 years. He let her go but she took everything with her. Berni knew he could not harass her, he had to let her think.

Esmeralda appeared very early in front of the building where the Insurance Company was located, but Berni had been there for an hour before. She was radiantly beautiful. When she looked at him she smiled and he reciprocated. "Wait for me at the same table where we were before. How long will it take you?" "No more than half an hour," Esmeralda answered. She crossed the street and entered the building. Berni sat in the same place. Meanwhile he was thinking about everything he had planned. Exactly half an hour passed and she entered and sat in the chair that Berni pulled out for her. They were face to face again. Berni looked into her eyes and said, "My God, how I love you." She waited and Berni fell silent. The silence could be heard, it seemed that all those present agreed. They joined their lips and lost themselves in a kiss. Tears flowed from their eyes, but they were joyful tears that bounced on the table.

Minutes passed and they did not realize that the establishment's employee had already passed twice. Berni offered apologies to the waitress and gave her the order to bring them a margarita and a beer. Meanwhile, Berni was telling Esmeralda that with her he gave value to life and now felt again the desire to live. "Now I have faith."

"I want to cry," said Esmeralda. "Cry, my love." "I am not the one you knew, I am a mother and I owe myself to them." She broke into tears, tears of pain. Berni handed her his perfumed handkerchief. Crying, she said to him, "It's the same lotion!" "Yes, it's the same, you are the same, I am the same, our love is the same."

Berni changed the subject to avoid another crisis.

Esmeralda asked him the time and upon learning it was 10 o'clock she stood up. "When will we see each other again?" He did not dare ask for her phone number. "I have to come back on Friday. Wait for me here at the same time as today!" "I will wait for you."

Berni waited a few minutes and went to the insurance office to ask for her. "She was in our offices two hours ago but will return on Friday." "Good, thank you very much," said Berni.

Esmeralda went straight to the university and there asked a friend if she could pick her up at her house in the afternoon to tell her something very important. After attending to her children, she left at nightfall for Rocio's house. There she told her everything about Berni, from the first day she met him at the company they worked for, until today's meeting. To the million-dollar question, she answered yes. "I still love him." "You must be sure why he comes looking for you now, could it be," added Rocio, emphasizing, "that his love is for the money you received? For the 500 million pesos from the insurance they paid you?" Esmeralda was frightened. She never thought of that. However, she answered that "she knew that Berni was never interested in fortune." "I know very well that he had many opportunities to have money and never appreciated them. In the United States he could have been one of the great drug mafia figures and he did not accept. They sought him to direct drug trafficking and he preferred to work as a number man in factories or parking lots."

Esmeralda left after having agreed to see Rocio again.

Esmeralda was driving her car toward her house and while doing so she was thinking about not attending Friday's next appointment with Berni. "That way, I can dedicate myself to my children just as I promised. It may be that Berni really came only for the money and that money is not mine, it is my children's."

On another side of the city, Berni was leaving the long-distance call office from where he had communicated with his wife Lilian to tell her that the money was about to be lost and that she should wait a few more days because they would possibly pay him before the merger of the two banks. This was false. The capital invested by Berni was not at any risk and besides, friend of insurance as he always was, he had a bank bankruptcy risk policy. So he would never have a considerable loss, apart from some interest losses due to the chess system that caused the drops in the New York stock markets.

He also went to present himself at the International Banking Company, where they had been waiting for him for two weeks. This multinational had an important position that was offered to him from Miami. When he arrived at the offices, they immediately invited him to lunch, where they would explain all the work he would do within the branch. The salary they offered him would be US$5,000.00 equivalent to 12,000,000.00 million Colombian pesos.

This proposal was accepted by Berni but he asked for one more week to take possession of his position, under the pretext of needing a little time to find an apartment and a car to rent. The company did not object and instead offered him a suite or room that it owned in one of the best hotels in the city. Berni thanked them for the generous gesture but refused the favor. Twenty years abroad served to teach him not to accept favors from his employers.

Everything was in order and this brought Berni good rest.

Everything was set to sustain a serious, unconditional and secure relationship for Esmeralda. Berni's intentions were clear. And at least for now, Berni had no intentions of a sexual relationship with Esmeralda. This he could assure. And he would make it known to her, once he saw her again, for which he was counting the minutes, hours and days. He slept little and woke up startled to look at the calendar looking for Friday to dawn.

For Berni it was a vital necessity to be near her, and he would wait a little longer to have her in his still strong arms and give her all his love drop by drop. He waited 30 years and one more would make no difference.

Meanwhile, the insurance company called Esmeralda by phone to announce that her check was ready. "Can I come right now?" she asked, to which the manager replied yes. "I'll wait for you with pleasure." It was a Thursday morning; one day before the day longed for by Berni. He had bought himself a new dress, went to the salon and had his hair done, his fingernails, and for the first time, they cut his toenails. He had always done this himself. That day was the most important for him. It was as special as those when he met each of his children.

At six in the morning he was at the same door of the entrance to the building. In front of the place where they had been meeting each week. Berni could not avoid the trembling of his body. He looked at himself in the glass windows and posed like a model. "I look good," he said to himself. Right after the entrance he noticed a bookstore and this gave him great joy. "How good," he thought, "that bookstores have not yet ended." He looked at some works and promised himself to buy two books when they opened. Among others were "The Narco Prosecutor" and "The Tin Drum." When he saw the prices he thought that governments should subsidize the costs, to give the majority access to reading. "In this same window I am going to see my book very soon and I myself am subsidizing it, as I made known to my respectable and honorable literary agent."

On Berni's watch it was 9 in the morning. He felt that his heart was stopping. One, two and three hours passed. Berni was distraught. He crossed the street and entered the cafeteria and looked toward the table that witnessed their love, he spread his gaze to all sides, he went to the ladies' room and opened the door. There was no one there. He asked the girl who always served them. Then each of the waitresses. "But how is it that you haven't seen her?" He almost shouted. "No sir, I haven't seen her, she hasn't come for days." He ran out and went to the insurance office and asked the secretary for her. "No sir, she hasn't come today," she answered. "Please check in the other offices!" "No sir, she cannot be inside without having passed in front of me." He left and waited for the elevator and since it took more than a minute, he went down the stairs jumping every three steps. Outside, at the door, there was a lottery seller and he asked him about her. "No sir, I don't know that lady. I have seen many women like that, but I don't know who Esmeralda is," the man said. "You're wrong! There are no women like her," Berni snapped very close to his face. "All right, sir," the lottery seller replied. "Buy a lottery ticket from me, it's good for you. He who has no luck in love, has it in gambling." Berni had already moved away from the place and did not hear the advice.

He walked without knowing where he was going. He went up the street and on his way back passed again in front of the building and looked inside the cafeteria. He returned at noon, minutes before the insurance company closed and now calmer asked the proper question. "Excuse me. When can Mrs. Esmeralda come to pick up the check?" "She picked it up yesterday!" That was the answer that for Berni was a sentence. He left again and went to pick up his car.

He headed south and reached the university. He parked his car and waited.

Esmeralda had to come pick up her daughter and he would be there to ask her; a woman can break a promise to a man, but a mother never leaves a child waiting. Berni repeated this to himself while waiting. There were almost two hours left before the students left. Meanwhile, and without taking his eyes off the driver of each car that arrived, he began to write. He started with a title without thinking. "The New Toy of Fools." A very mismatched couple, he a fat man or rather pot-bellied, with a rogue's face, with a top hat and dressed elegantly, wearing a tie with the flags of all countries, was standing waiting for the bullet train that would take him through all the Central American and South American towns. The station of the fastest express in the world was in Mexico and from there would depart the famous character who by the way spoke very strange Spanish, but was a native of the United States of North America. His name, according to a journalist who wanted to interview him, was Mr. Alalc. Apparently, he wanted to sell the image of progress in the carnivals that would take place in those days, called "Global Carnival." She was a very thin woman, her face showed traces of suffering. Her dress was old but clean. She wandered around the station and when she saw the fat man and his entourage she went after him, as she was uglier than Betty, the fat man paid her no attention. She took advantage of the organizers' carelessness and got on the train. When the drunk friend of hers, with whom she was always seen, shouted "Poverty, Poverty, don't leave me, give me your hand," she grabbed him and in a matter of seconds they were already camouflaged in a seat in the last car of the train. "Don't worry," the drunk told Poverty, "we know those lands very well, so we can get there and these distinguished gentlemen of the troupe, when they realize our presence, it will be too late." "Yes, yes," added Poverty. "They are going to distract the people with their new toy and we will live our lives quietly. Have a drink but we have to take care of it, because the trip will last until 2005." At that moment, Berni looked up and saw when Esmeralda's car parked right next to him. He got out and went to her and opening the door, said, "Good afternoon, distinguished lady. Can you tell me what happened this morning?" "Oh, my God. I am so sorry but I didn't have a phone number to call you, those things that I forgot to ask you for. Well, what happened is that only yesterday I closed a contract for an apartment. By the way, I want to invite you to see it. Of course if time permits." "Look, Berni," Esmeralda was saying in a grave voice. "What we have cannot be, it is impossible." "But my love," said Berni. And Esmeralda interrupted him. "Yesterday, when my children found me crying in my room, they called me to account and forced me to give them an explanation. They had been observing my attitude and noticed that I was very nervous and cried every day; from the first day we saw each other you and I. I promised them again that I would not attend to another man or rather, that I would not accept your relationship, not as a friend, boyfriend or lover and much less as a husband. I spoke to them about you and they did not accept any explanation. When I told them that I still loved you they gave me the alternative: us or him, Mom. Now you can see that I have no other way but to end this dream. Let me live like this, as I always lived from the day you left my side."

"Please my love. This is now a reality. You no longer have your husband and that's why I didn't present myself to you before. Allow me at least to be near, as friends, if you prefer. There is no one now in your heart, accept me!" "You are wrong, you are in my heart but only that, in my heart. I repeat Berni, it cannot be and please never look for me again."

"Wait, let's see each other again at the cafeteria, this afternoon after you leave your daughter at home." "All right, we'll see each other there. Thank you Esmeralda. I'll wait for you."

She got out of the car and went to pick up her daughter who was watching from the balcony of the university. Berni started his car and went to the city center. He parked near the agreed place and walked, passing in front of the church of Las Mercedes, which he had never visited before, he entered and knelt. "Your Grace. Grant me the grace to appease Esmeralda's spirit. Do not allow my presence to cause her pain, problems or conflict. Tell her ear that I have returned with the best intentions I never had for any woman." He left and went to the cafeteria. There he felt safer and indeed, he sat at the same table where he had given Esmeralda a kiss, that kiss he waited 30 years for. The most sublime and loving kiss that anyone ever gave to anyone.

He called the waitress, the same as before, and asked for a bottle of French Brandy. When the girl—she was between 20 and 30 years old—served him, he thanked her with a five-dollar bill but asked for another glass. "With pleasure, sir." And in a few minutes she was back. "If you want to toast with me, come closer." She approached and together they raised their glasses. "Who is the toast for?" asked the waitress. "For the most beautiful woman in the universe," said Berni, winking at her. She smiled, taking it personally.

Meanwhile, time passed, shots of brandy passed to Berni's head. For every three he drank, the employee who served him drank one. The young woman spoke to him about a soccer match that would take place that night. "The regional classic," she said. But Berni listened but did not hear her. His senses were all at the entrance door to the cafeteria and his eyes seemed larger than normal. Berni knew that it was already time for Esmeralda to be there with him, but she was not. He had contained the desire to look at the time but could no longer. It was 6 in the afternoon.

Berni was falling apart, not from the effect of alcohol in his blood, because he was very resistant, but because doubt was overwhelming him. Disillusionment had attacked him and was tearing him to pieces. He began to drink more and the anguish was greater. Now he understood what Esmeralda told him three hours before. Her words were hammering in his brain. He felt guilty for all the evils of humanity. While reflecting, the young girl sat down and he did not notice. She said to him, "Thank you for waiting for me. I already delivered my things"—she had finished her work—"and I am available from now on." "Thank you, you are very attentive and charming," said Berni and added, "What do you think about a love date, when the lady does not show up to keep it?" She answered, "When a woman loves a man, she never leaves him waiting." This new sentence left Berni imprisoned in his disgrace.

The plane departed at 9:30 in the morning on Saturday bound for the Capital of the Sun. Miami. On the passenger list was Berni. They offered him liquor and he did not accept. "No, I am not going to drink. I return home, to the side of my children, they are first and after, anything else. Yes, I return to give my company and the love I have left, to that woman who has always loved me, without caring to receive anything in return, to the one who knows me and accepts me as I am and who has always trusted me. She, faithful and self-sacrificing. I am going to accept the will of God by letting destiny take my Esmeralda away again and now forever. I can no longer go back on her path, I will never be able to reach her. I have to accept the payment for my mistakes."

From the airport, Berni called his wife and she with a joy that could be heard in the telephone cord, went out to receive him in the company of her beloved son Marco Antonio. In full flight Berni thought that now it was not necessary to go in search of his children as it always corresponded to him to do because with computer technology, he would be seeing them in the middle of the conversation. He thought, now we parents and grandparents will not suffer so much waiting for our children and grandchildren. These advances in technology let us enter their homes without them even realizing it. "Yes, it is correct. One day, very soon, I will enter Esmeralda's room and tell her that I love her like no other, without her children being able to prevent it."

Berni had become an exemplary husband and father and a worker of many carats.

The swallow friend of the "Happy Prince," by author Oscar Wilde. "Return Lord my Spirit to the people in need of love, health, company and justice. My time is up. What? What did I just say to you? Oh my God. Now I remember that time is like You who alleviates all pain and suffering. Of course, time is You yourself and that is what I need. My problems will be solved with the time You give me to solve them. Perfect!"

Berni found in his encounter with God, the greatest treasure that exists.

Berni thought he had found the greatest treasure that would save his life. That would save him from the lack of love he had been feeling.

Pirate Morgan, there on the Island of San Andres, in Colombia; never came to have the treasure that Berni now had.

At that very moment, Berni thought, that if his Father, Don Marco Aurelio and his Brother Cesar, the tailor, had spoken with God, surely He would have saved them from suicide by speaking to them about time. "What a shame. It is a matter of waiting a moment until it heals the wounds that make us bleed out. In a few months or years, all problems disappear. Why not wait. The life of humans is 6 million years old. So why not wait a few seconds that are really needed within the millions of years of existence?"

Why do people let themselves be carried away by problems or emotions, until they reach suicide, cause the death of others, separate from their partner, abandon the family as if from these acts would result the solution that torments them.

"It took me longer to lower my arms and bow my head before you, Our Father."

IN THE END, Berni resolved, definitively to crucify his other SELF.

He was going to let this one die, thus letting the true Berni replace him.

He had read a work by the famous Paulo Coelho, Nobel of Literature, in which Berni after reading it, took the idea that he now proposed. Coelho cites the woman who leaves her sedentary life, her studies, her dreams, her profession, to go in search of the OTHER, the one she had been observing for several months, the one who invited her to enjoy life, its charms, her youthful love.

Only in Berni, this effect was the opposite. Berni abandons the OTHER, which is precisely the one that prevents him from a sedentary, peaceful life, without adventures, women, dreams of greatness. That other of Him, who could never oppose this one, the unfaithful, ambitious, proud and unconcerned about things of value like love, respect, honesty and fidelity.

Then, a while later, Berni went to the library in search of a book to read and found one titled: EVERYTHING A MAN SHOULD KNOW ABOUT WOMEN.

He paid for it and went to sit in a chair. He opened the book and to his surprise, it was blank. It contained nothing on its pages, this caused him so much admiration, that he took it to his house and placed it on the shelves of his library. "Incredible," he thought, "without being written, it says everything we know or know about Women. NOTHING."

Jesus at the last supper clearly separates the body from the Spirit, and invites us to live eternal life, through true repentance.

Berni says: "Lord Jesus Christ, I am repentant in my heart for having offended you and I detest from now on my offenses and sins. From now on I will do your will, not mine."

Father: I feel the joy of those who are safe on earth and of those who in pure Spirit, surround our lives, the Planet, the Spiritual Universe and the Cosmos.

THE END

www.ingramcontent.com/pod-product-compliance
Lightning Source LLC
Chambersburg PA
CBHW061740120626
46550CB00005B/1840